No Needles Knitting

Easy Techniques and Projects for Making Quick and Cozy Modern Knits by Hand

VICKIE MONTOYA HOWELL

Quarto.com

First Published in 2025 by Quarry Books, an imprint of The Quarto Group,
100 Cummings Center, Suite 265-D, Beverly, MA 01915, USA.
T (978) 282-9590 F (978) 283-2742

EEA Representation, WTS Tax d.o.o.,
Žanova ulica 3, 4000 Kranj, Slovenia.
www.wts-tax.si

29 28 27 26 3 4 5

ISBN: 978-0-7603-9675-9

Digital edition published in 2025
eISBN: 978-0-7603-9676-6

Library of Congress Cataloging-in-Publication Data is available.

Photography: Traci Goudie
Models: Clover Campbell, Tristan Howell, Vickie Howell,
Sowmya Kulukuru, Milo McKinney, Azula Thiam
Tech Editing: Lori Steinberg
Schematics: Tristan Howell
Illustrations: Clover Campbell
French Knot Diagram (page 84): Becky Joiner

Printed in Huizhou City, Guangdong, China TT022026

To all of the teenagers and young adults who started finger knitting with me a decade ago and are now ready to level up their creations. Here's to creating your own style—for body and space—and making your unique mark in this world!

Contents

Self 31

projects to wear

Space 81

projects for where you dwell

Introduction

In the decades that I've been a fiber crafter, the thing that continues to excite me most is watching the ways that yarn crafts continue to morph and return to shape—to retract and expand. The techniques and skills created by our foremothers a millennium ago continuously reinvent themselves to suit the temperament of trends, societal state of consciousness, and innovation or exploration of materials at hand. What's old is new; what's new is old. These cycles, looping around and through, show a resilience fueled by creativity.

Right now, we're in this paradoxical time when people are going back to grounding traditions—cooking, mending, hand-making—but with the help of technology like social media, video platforms, and AI to inform, inspire, and innovate. For better or worse we're all in this together, and I for one am here for it all. I love mixing the past with the present—juxtaposing what always was with what could be, especially when it comes to creating.

Years ago when I wrote *Finger Knitting Fun*, for which this book is the unofficial sequel, my goal was to encourage kids to see fiber as a blank canvas for self-expression. To motivate them with the alchemy of turning string into something else altogether. To empower them with the knowledge that if they wanted to give a gift, or needed something warm to wear, they can produce it themselves. Once those fundamentals are set, then the fun really begins. Enter *No Needles Knitting*.

As I began to think about how the cords created by finger knitting could evolve into something more versatile for stitchers who themselves are also evolving into young adults and beyond, I jumped into the frenzied activity on TikTok. Much to my delight, I found expanded definitions of "finger" knitting—the creation of flat panels of fabric made with hands and extremely thick yarns. TikTok users were knitting, but without needles! By laying rows of loops over loops of Jumbo yarn they were, in fact, hand-knitting garments in a flash! I knew I could translate any simple technique created with needled knitting into this version of the craft. The world was my needle-less oyster!

So this book's creation began and joyously continued, by playing with scale (see Building Block Blanket on page 99, Posh Pallet on page 103, and Cushy Life on page 107), redefining fast fashion (see Cozeplay on page 33, Vest Is Best on page 69, and Chain-gling necklace on page 73), and experimenting with alternative mediums (Tee Tote-ler Bag on page 55, Frame in Lights on page 119, and Weave, Not Waste on page 121). The result is a collection of projects and tutorials intended to act as an invitation to you, maker-friend, to go big with your creativity, super-size your view of stitching, and conjure up pieces that express the uniquely beautiful you.

Have fun!

Vickie

1973

Getting Started

choosing yarns and how-tos for knitting without needles

The Right Puff

Knitting without needles works best with supersize yarns—either ones that exist, or those made by double-, triple-, or quadruple-stranding multiple yarns together. When shopping for yarns, though, I'd recommend looking at the labels (or online descriptions) for the following three weight categories (aka thickness) of yarns.

Tip

Learn more about yarn types and weights at yarnstandards.com.

SUPER BULKY

JUMBO

GIANT

what's your type?

You can finger- and hand-knit with any type of yarn, but there are definitely some that really shine.

ROVING YARNS

This is a single-ply yarn with lots of loft. It's usually made from wool and has a beautiful "bloom"—meaning it expands to fill the space between stitches when knit. The downside is that it's relatively delicate. Since there aren't plies to keep it together, the fibers can break easily, so this yarn isn't ideal for anything that will get a lot of wear and tear.

TUBE YARNS

To me, these are the yarns that were made for knitting without needles. They consist of a fabric tube (jersey, velveteen, polyester, etc.), filled with polyester fiberfill. They'd be too weighty on the wrists to work well with knitting needles, but they thrive when knit up with hands. They make really cushy projects and are especially perfect for home decor items.

CHENILLE-STYLE YARNS

Primarily made out of polyester, these yarns are very strong but also soft and fuzzy. They work well for anything cozy and are easy to find because most craft yarn companies make them.

gauge the difference

Gauge is the measurement of how many stitches and rows you get per inch when you knit. Although it's not crucial for many of the projects in this book, and it's a little harder to determine gauge than in traditional knitting because there aren't needles involved to regulate stitch sizes, knowing these measurements becomes important when you want something to fit (like a sweater or hat).

Gauge also affects how much yarn you'll need for a project. The standard system for gauge measurement is using a 4" (10 cm) swatch. Don't feel like you need to get bogged down by the numbers for any of the projects in the book, but if you notice that your Cozeplay cardi (see page 33) seems ginormous, or your Twister headband (page 67) is knitting up too small, check your gauge against what's listed in the pattern. If you're way off, then consider making smaller or larger loops and stitches.

Not to worry, though. Mostly you can adjust the sizing of your item by adding or subtracting chains in your foundation row, then knitting from there. Practice makes perfect . . . but also, this craft doesn't need to be perfect. The most important thing is that you're having fun and feeling great about putting something positive out into the maker-world!

Other Supplies

For a successful no-needles knitting experience, here are a few items that are helpful to keep within reach.

- **A large table to work at.** When all else fails, the floor does work, but your back will thank you if you can do the lion's share of your knitting without having to stoop over. Psst . . . don't forget to take stretching breaks!
- **Measuring tape.** Either a retractable tape or a tailor's version will work. You just need something that's long enough to measure large pieces, and flexible enough to measure circumferences.
- **Yarn needle with an extra-large eye.** Big yarns require a big needle. Although most ends can be woven in and most projects in this book can be seamed with fingers, it's nice to have the option of a needle for finishing, especially when working with fuzzier yarns.
- **Long pipe cleaners.** These work great as stitch holders for when you need to set aside your project before it's bound off. Simply slide one through the live stitches, then twist the ends together to hold.
- **Large sewing or binder clips.** When seaming two pieces together, it's useful to have something to hold them in place as you go. You can purchase clips made especially for this purpose at a craft store or online. Alternatively, just raid the office supplies section for binder clips. Whatever helps you to grab a grip is good with me!

Hand Knitting

foundation chain

Ironically, every hand-knit project begins not by knitting at all, but rather by finger crocheting a chain. Here's how:

1. Leaving a 6" (15 cm) tail for weaving in later, make slipknot by folding the yarn in a loop-de-loop (with the *working* yarn, aka the yarn connected to the ball) on top.
2. Bring the working yarn under the loop, then push it through, creating a new loop.
3. Pull so knot is taut, but loop is still large enough to fit over two of your fingers.
4. Place the slipknot loop over your "pincher" fingers (thumb and forefinger). Pull the working yarn through the loop.
5. One chain stitch created.
6. Continue pulling a working yarn loop through the loop on your fingers, until chain is desired length (or number of stitches).

hand-knit stitch

The knit stitch is the fundamental stitch for hand knitting. In fact, when repeated, it creates what you probably think of when you think of a knit item. Within the context of hand knitting, in which we're working back and forth on the right side (front) of a piece, repeating the knit stitch creates what traditionally is called a stockinette stitch (see below). Combined with other stitches, though, it's a building block for all kinds of stitches and stitch patterns.

1. A knit stitch, whether worked in a foundation chain or in existing knit rows of live stitches, is worked the same. With the working yarn in back, pull a loop through the stitch (live loop or chain) below.
2. Knit stitch created.
3. Continue pulling a loop through each individual stitch until row is complete.

What's in a Name?

If you do an internet search, you may find knitting without needles called different things: finger knitting, loop knitting, hand knitting, table knitting, etc. To further confuse the issue, post–industrial revolution the term "hand knit" has meant anything that was knit with handheld needles versus a garment that was machine knit. There's also an argument to be made that all needle-less knitting uses fingers. For the purposes of this book (and in historical relation to traditional knitting techniques), "finger knitting" is the method of creating long tubes of fabric, beginning by weaving yarn around fingers. "Hand knitting" begins with a foundation chain and is the method of creating flat pieces of fabric. Either way, have fun!

Hand Knitting (continued)

stockinette stitch

Stockinette stitch, the fabric one commonly thinks of when describing knitting, is created by knitting every row as follows:

1. Lay your foundation chain on a flat surface, with the smooth side facing up.
2. **Row 1:** Working from **right** to **left**, and with the working yarn in back, pull a loop through the second chain from the loop (that "live" loop counts as your first stitch). Two knit stitches made.
3. Continue pulling a loop through each individual chain across to end. Row complete. Do not turn work.
4. **Row 2:** Working from **left** to **right** and with the working yarn in back, pull a loop through each individual loop across to end.
5. **Row 3:** Working from **right** to **left** and with the working yarn in back, pull a loop through each individual loop across to end.
6. Repeat Rows 2–3 to create stockinette stitch.

hand-purl stitch

The purl stitch is the yang to the knit stitch yin. It's literally the opposite of the knit stitch, resulting in a little bump on the fabric. Worked alone, or combining in different ways with its sister stitch, any number of textural patterns can be created. Once you know how to knit and purl, you can basically knit any pattern that exists. Go, you!

1. A purl stitch, whether worked in a foundation chain or in existing knit or purled rows of live stitches, is worked the same. With the working yarn in front, push a loop through the stitch (live loop or chain) below.
2. Purl stitch created.
3. Continue pushing a loop, from front to back, through each individual stitch, until row is complete.

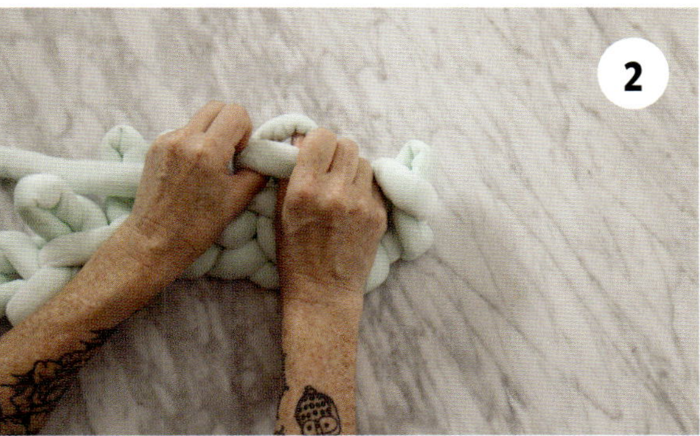

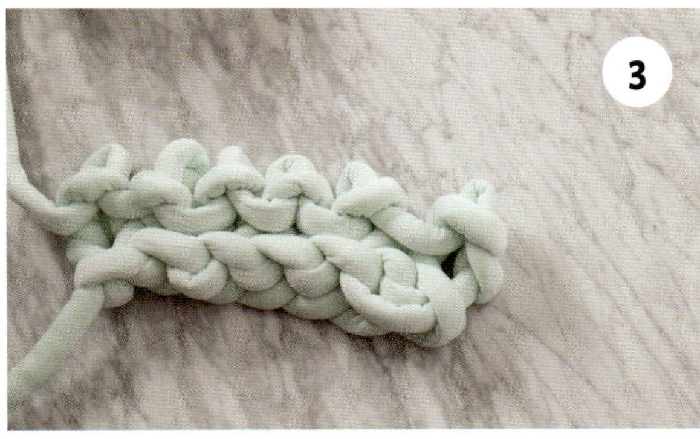

Maintaining Consistent Loop Height

The height you pull the loop to may vary based on weight (thickness) of yarn. Usually, anywhere from 1½–2" (3.8 to 5 cm) is good. Experiment with what works best with your chosen yarn, then try to maintain evenness in loop height throughout.

Hand Knitting (continued)

hand-knit garter stitch

Garter stitch for hand knitting is created by alternating rows of knit stitches with rows of purl stitches as follows:

1. Start with steps 1 and 2 for stockinette stitch (see page 14). With the working yarn in front and working from left to right, purl stitches across to end.
2. With working yarn in back and working from right to left, knit the stitches across to end.
3. Repeat steps 3–4 to create garter stitch.

1

2

3

joining a new ball or color

Joining a new ball of yarn happens when you either want to change colors or need to start a new ball of the same color. It should always be done at the beginning of a row (to prevent holes) and leaving at least a 6" (15 cm) tail (for both new and old yarns) for weaving in later. Since many of the yarns used in hand knitting specifically are very bulky, it's sometimes useful to start a new ball on the opposite end from where you finished the last time. This will prevent unnecessary distortion of the fabric potentially caused by chunky ends all being woven in on the same side.

1. Leave a 6" (15 cm) tail laying next to the side of the project that you're joining.
2. Begin knitting with new yarn.

Note: The tails of both old and new yarns may need to be tugged on a bit to tighten the first or last stitch made.

1

2

hand-knit cable

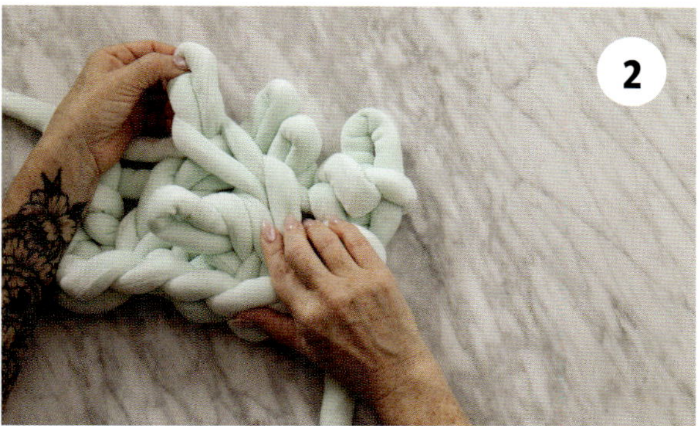

Cables are crossed stitches that create a pretzel-like twist in the fabric. They're magical to make and are a great, elevating technique when added to a plain fabric. Generally, they're worked over a bed of reverse stockinette stitch, which in hand knitting means purling every row. The smaller bumps of the purls support the boldness of the cable. In traditional knitting, cables can be made with any number of stitches, but at the scale we're working with in this book, I recommend working over four stitches.

1. Work the number of plain stitches called for in the pattern. Skip first two stitches, letting the live loops carefully fall to the FRONT of the work; knit next two stitches (taking care not to pull the yarn out of the previous loops).
2. Knit the two skipped loops.
3. Left-leaning cable made.

Right-leaning Cable

Should you want your cable to lean right instead of left, repeat the above process but instead hold the unworked stitches to the BACK of the work, instead of the FRONT.

Increases

knit front & back

This method increases your stitch count by one. It produces a purl bump, so it's ideal for projects worked in garter stitch.

1. Knit the designated stitch.
2. Working in the SAME stitch, purl. One stitch increased.

make 1

As with its knit front and back counterpart, one stitch is increased with this method. This version produces a flatter, less noticeable new stitch. There will, however, usually be a small hole created. This hole is often used decoratively to create eyelets in a pattern while increasing.

3. Lift the bar IN BETWEEN the stitch you've just worked and the next stitch.
4. Knit that bar as if it were a loop. One stitch increased.

Decreases

knit 2 together

This method decreases a stitch. The direction it slants depends on whether the outer stitch being decreased is placed on top or underneath the inner stitch. If the way the stitch slants doesn't matter for the project, then pick yer poison—either one gets the decreasing job done!

knit 2 together—left

1. Lay the outer loop (stitch) on the bottom of the next stitch.
2. Knit two stitches together as if they were one. One stitch decreased.

knit 2 together—right

1. Lay the outer loop (stitch) on top of the next stitch.
2. Knit two stitches together as if they were one. One stitch decreased.

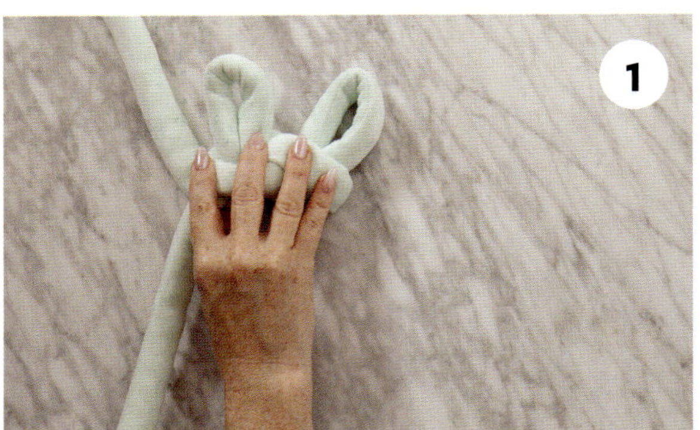

i-cord

I-cord creates a long tube, much like finger knitting, but without requiring the yarn to be wrapped around your fingers. This method is a great choice when using Jumbo (#7) or Giant (#8) yarns, or when applying it to a project for a piping effect.

1. Create a foundation chain of two stitches (or as many as the pattern calls for).
2. Pull up loop in the second chain.
3. Bring the strand from the left-hand side behind the live loops and knit the rightmost stitch first.
4. Then, knit the leftmost stitch.
5. Bring the strand from the right-hand side behind the live loops and knit the leftmost stitch first. Then, knit the rightmost stitch.
6. After working a few rows, you'll begin to notice the cord forming by the outer edges being pulled in from the process. Continue as established for as long as you'd like your cord.

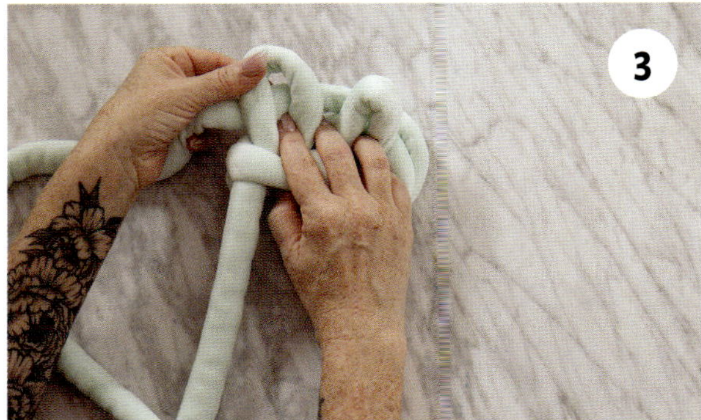

binding off

1. Knit two stitches as normal.
2. Pass the first stitch over the second so the loop is no longer "live." One stitch is bound off.
3. Knit the next stitch.
4. Pass the first stitch over the second stitch.
5. Repeat the last two steps until one stitch remains; cut yarn, leaving a tail.
6. Feed tail through last loop and pull taut.
7. Leave long tail for weaving in or seaming per the project pattern's instruction.

Finger Knitting

Finger knitting creates long, tubed strands. The girth of these strands can change based on thickness of yarn and number of fingers you weave over. Because your fingers always hold the live loops, it's easier to get even stitches than, perhaps, hand knitting. Finger knitting also allows you to use a bit thinner yarns than its hand-y counterpart. Conversely, even the largest of hands would struggle to finger knit with Giant yarns. Like all handicrafts, each type of knitting has a space in which it thrives. Have fun experimenting!

finger knitting strands

1. Leaving a 6" (15 cm) tail for weaving in later, lay the yarn across the palm of your nondominant hand and between the pointer and middle fingers.
2. Using your dominant hand, wrap the yarn counterclockwise around the pointer finger on your nondominant hand.
3. Weave the yarn under and over the next three (or number required for pattern) fingers (middle, pointer, and pinky).
4. Bring the yarn up and around your pinky finger and weave it back in the opposite direction over the next three fingers (ring, middle, and pointer). You'll now have loose yarn on all fingers, excluding the thumb.
5. Lay the yarn across your fingers, above the loops.
6. Lift your pointer finger loop over the yarn and let it drop off your finger.
7. Continuing as in step 6, lift the loop over the yarn and let it drop off the ring, middle, and pointer fingers. You've just completed the first row!
8. Repeat steps 5–7 until your finger-knitted cord is the desired length.

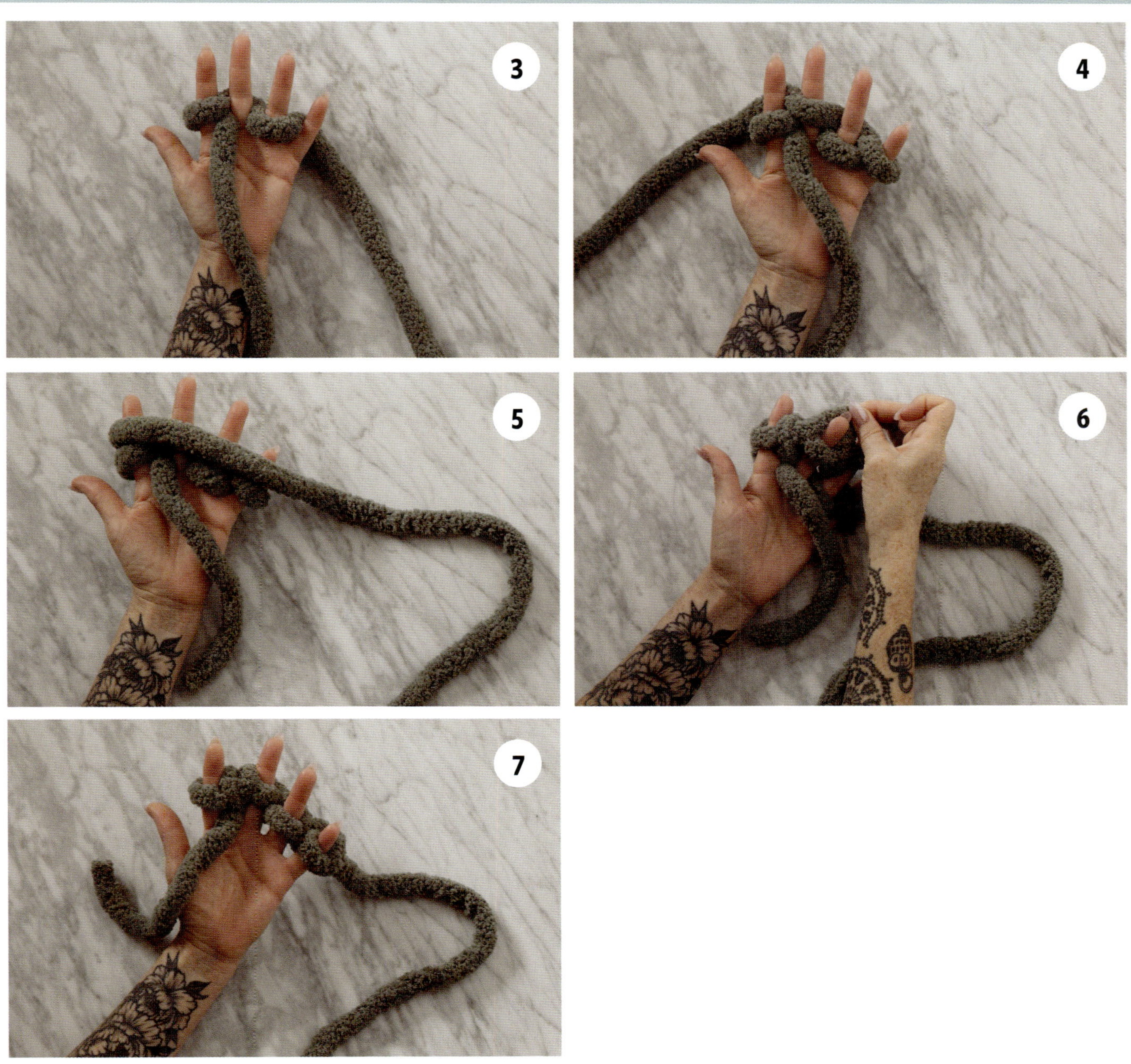

Finger Knitting (continued)

fastening off

Fastening off is how a finger-knit piece is removed from the stitcher's hand, cleanly so that it doesn't unravel.

1. Finger knit stitches on your first two fingers.
2. Remove loop from first finger and place on the next finger. You'll now have two stacked loops on that finger.
3. Pull bottom loop over top loop and let it drop off that finger.
4. Finger knit stitch on the next finger.
5. Repeat step 2.
6. Repeat steps 4–5 until 1 loop remains.
7. Cut yarn, leaving a 6" (15 cm) tail. Take last loop off of your finger, feed the tail through loop (a), and pull snug (b).

For additional tips, tutorials, and bonus content, please scan the QR code to visit the *No Needles Knitting* playlist.

Feeling Loopy?

When hand knitting, you may wonder how big to make the loops. While the most important thing is to stay as consistent as possible, it's also useful to remember that the size of the loop will vary depending on the weight of yarn you're using. In other words, the thicker the yarn, the longer the loops will be. A good starting point is to try 1" (2.5 cm) tall for Super Bulky (#6), 1½–2" (4–5 cm) for Jumbo (#7), and 2–2½" (5–6 cm) for Giant (#8) yarns. Trust your eye, though. Depending on the type of yarn (and its fluffiness, or lack thereof), you may need to adjust.

Finger Crochet

Finger crochet is useful when a sculptural element is desired. Ironically, the foundation row that all hand-knitting projects start with is actually a finger-crocheted chain. For the purposes of this book, though, additional crochet techniques are only used to add dimension to a couple of projects. Here's what you'll need to know.

single crochet

1. With the loop from the last stitch worked still on your fingers, insert fingers in appropriate chain.
2. Pull up another loop (2 loops on fingers).
3. Wrap the yarn over your fingers and pull through BOTH loops.
4. Single crochet stitch complete.

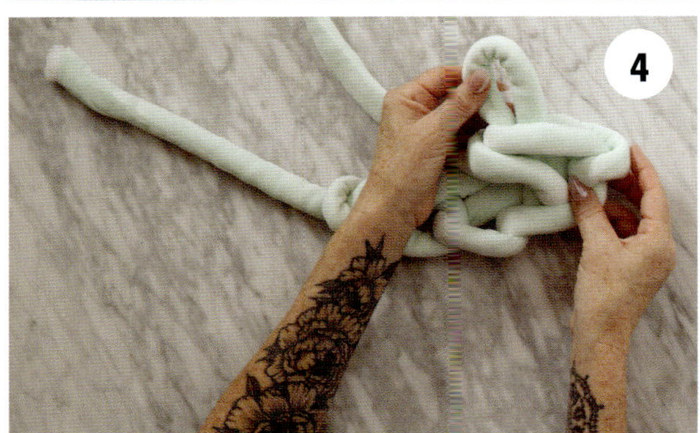

picot stitch

1. Work a single crochet stitch.
2. Chain three stitches.
3. Slip a stitch in the 3rd chain from your fingers by inserting your fingers through it (you'll now have two loops), then pull the yarn through both loops.
4. Picot stitch complete.

Finishing Techniques

weaving in ends

Weaving in ends is crucial so that your project doesn't begin to unravel, creating holes. You'll always do at least a little weaving in for most projects, although with some Jumbo and all Giant yarns, you may need to opt out of this method (for those, see the pattern instructions on sewing the ends down).

1. Using a yarn needle with an extra-large eye or your fingers, weave tail in and out of stitches on the wrong side of your work for at least 6" (15 cm).
2. Gently tug on project so that the tail relaxes into the fabric; snip off any extra.

mattress stitch

Mattress stitch creates a barely visible seam and is one of the most-used seaming methods in knitting.

1. Lay two project pieces sitting parallel and with right sides facing.
2. Using a long strand of yarn and a yarn needle with an extra-large eye or your fingers, bring yarn up from back to front through one of the pieces where you'd like to start your seaming.
3. Next, draw the yarn under the bar (aka the ladder) between the two outermost stitches of the second knit piece, directly across from where you started on your first piece.
4. Bring the yarn under the bar between the first two stitches on the first piece. From here, you'll zigzag back and forth.
5. Continue in this manner, going back and forth between the two pieces and working in the bars between stitches, until piece is seamed.

Self

projects to wear

Cozeplay

chunky striped cardigan

Slow fashion doesn't have to take a long time to create! This super-chunky striped cardi can be made one day and worn the next. It'll keep you cozy and add a pop to your wardrobe.

MATERIALS

- Super Bulky yarn (#6), 100% wool (single ply), in two colors
  Shown: Knit Picks Tuff Puff (3.5 oz/100 g, 44 yd/40.3 m, 100% wool): 5 (6, 6, 7) balls Off White (A) and 5 (5, 6, 6) balls Cactus Blossom (B)
- Yarn needle with an extra-large eye

Note: This yarn is used holding 2 strands together (DOUBLE STRANDED) for this project. If substituting with a heavier weight yarn to be used single stranded, you'll need approximately 110 (132, 132, 154) yd [101 (121, 121, 141) m] of Color A and 110 (110, 132, 132) yd [101 (101, 121, 121) m] of Color B.

GAUGE

Approximately 4 stitches x 3½ rows = 4" (10 cm) in stockinette stitch, DOUBLE STRANDED, slightly stretched.

SIZES

1 (2, 3, 4)

FINISHED MEASUREMENTS

Bust: 42 (44, 48, 52)" [107 (112, 122, 132) cm]
Length: 17 (18, 19, 20)" [43 (46, 48, 51) cm]
This sweater is designed to have 6–8" (15.2–20.3 cm) of positive ease.

notes

- This project is worked with 2 strands of yarn held together throughout (DOUBLE STRANDED). Carry colors up along the side of work as you go.
- The project is worked with the right side facing you throughout. DO NOT TURN at the ends of rows.

Easy Does It

"Ease" refers to how tightly or loosely a garment fits the body.

- **Negative ease** is created by making a garment smaller than a body measurement with the intention for it to stretch to fit snugly.
- **Positive ease** occurs when a garment is made larger than a body measurement so that there's a draped, flowing, or flared effect.
- **No ease** means a garment is made to the exact measurements of the body without stretch or drape.

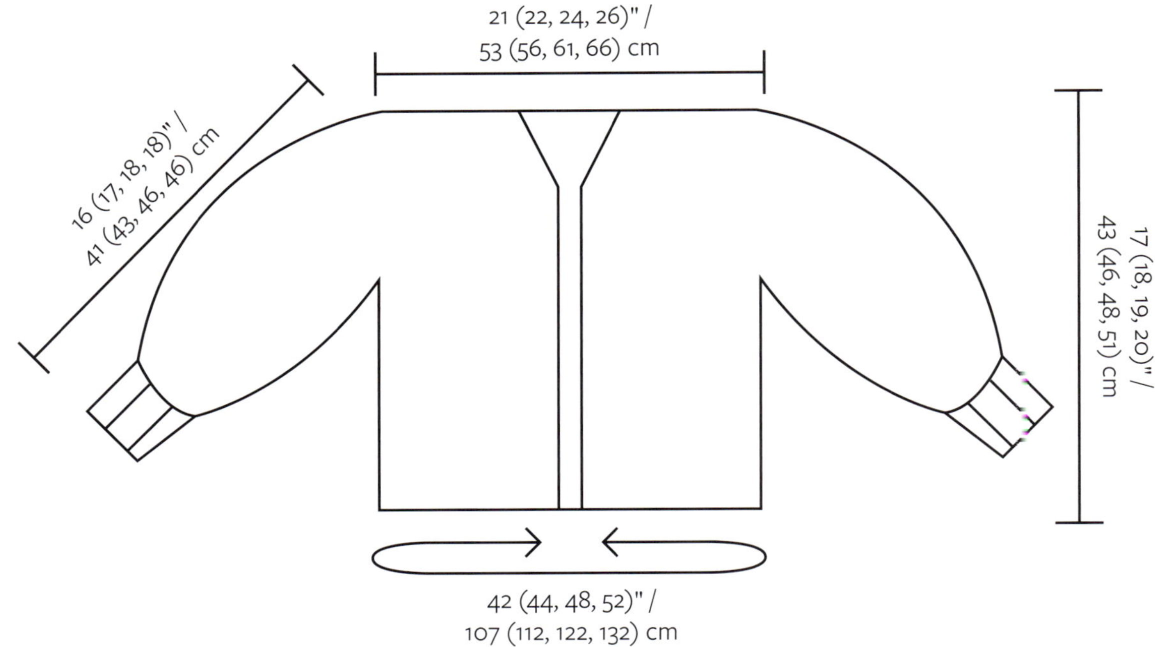

back

Foundation Row: With a DOUBLE STRAND of A, loosely chain 19 (20, 22, 24), or make a 21 (22, 24, 26)" [53 (56, 61, 66) cm] chain.
Row 1: With A, and working from right to left, pull up loop (stitch) in second chain, and every chain to the end of the row. Do not turn—20 (21, 23, 25) stitches for 21 (22, 24, 26)" [53 (56, 61, 66) cm].
Row 2: Working from left to right, knit every stitch to end of row.

Join DOUBLE STRAND of B.

Row 3: With B, working from right to left, knit every stitch to end of row.
Row 4: With B, working from left to right, knit every stitch to end of row.
Row 5: With A, working from right to left, knit every stitch to end of row.
Row 6: With A, working from left to right, knit every stitch to end of row.

Repeat Rows 3–6 for 2 (2, 2, 3) times MORE.

Note: For a cropped version, remove one repeat. For a longer version, add one or more repeats, keeping in mind that you might need more yarn.

With A, continue knitting every row until piece measures 17 (18, 19, 20)" [43 (46, 48, 51) cm] from edge.

Bind off.

left front

Foundation Row: With DOUBLE STRAND of A, loosely chain 9 (10, 11, 12), or make a 10½ (11, 12, 13)" [26.5 (28, 30.5, 33) cm] chain.
Row 1: With A and working from right to left, pull up loop (stitch) in second chain, and every chain to end. Do not turn—9 (10, 11, 12) stitches, or 10½ (11, 12, 13)" [26.5 (28, 30.5, 33) cm].
Row 2: Working from left to right, purl 1, knit in next stitch and knit every stitch to end of row.

Join DOUBLE STRAND of B.

Row 3: With B, working from right to left, knit every stitch to end of row.
Row 4: With B, working from left to right, purl 1, knit in next stitch and knit every stitch to end of row.
Row 5: With A, working from right to left, knit every stitch to end of row.
Row 6: With A, working from left to right, purl 1, knit in next stitch and knit every stitch to end of row.

Repeat Rows 3–6 for 2 (2, 2, 3) times MORE. Cut B.

With DOUBLE STRAND of A, repeat Rows 5 and 6 until piece measures 12 (13, 13, 14)" [30.5 (33, 33, 35.5) cm] from edge.

NECK SHAPING

Row 1: Working from right to left, knit to last 3 stitches, with second loop over next loop, knit 2 together (knit 2 together–right), purl 1—1 stitch decreased.
Row 2: Working from left to right, knit every stitch to end of row.

Repeat Rows 1 and 2 for 2 (2, 3, 3) times MORE—3 (3, 4, 4) stitches decreased total.

Continue in the pattern as established, knitting all stitches except for purled border stitch, for 2 rows, or until piece measures the same length as BACK.

Bind off, leaving long tail for seaming.

right front

Foundation Row: With DOUBLE STRAND of A, loosely chain 9 (10, 11, 12), or make a 10½ (11, 12, 13)" [26.5 (28, 30.5, 33) cm] chain.
Row 1: With A and working from right to left, pull up loop (stitch) in second chain, and every chain to end. Do not turn—9 (10, 11, 12) stitches, or 10½ (11, 12, 13)" [26.5 (28, 30.5, 33) cm].
Row 2: Working from left to right, knit every stitch to last stitch, purl 1.

Join DOUBLE STRAND of B.

Row 3: With B, working from right to left, knit every stitch to end of row.
Row 4: With B, working from left to right, purl 1, knit in the next stitch, knit every stitch to end of row.
Row 5: With A, working from right to left, knit every stitch to end of row.
Row 6: With A, working from left to right, knit every stitch to the last stitch, purl 1.

Repeat Rows 3–6 for 2 (2, 2, 3) times MORE. Cut B.

With DOUBLE STRAND of A, repeat Rows 5 and 6 until piece measures 12 (13, 13, 14)" [30.5 (33, 33, 35.5) cm] from edge.

NECK SHAPING

Row 1: Working from right to left, purl 1, place next loop over second loop and knit 2 together (knit 2 together–left), knit every stitch to end of row—1 stitch decreased.
Row 2: Working from left to right, knit every stitch to end of row.

Repeat Rows 1 and 2, for 2 (2, 3, 3) times MORE—3 (3, 4, 4) stitches decreased total.

Continue in the pattern as established, knitting all stitches except for the purled border stitch, for 2 rows, or until piece measures the same length as BACK.

Bind off, leaving long tail for seaming.

With fingers and using tails, seam LEFT and RIGHT FRONTS to BACK at shoulders.

sleeves (make 2)

With A, right side facing you, and beginning on the second color A row after last color B stripe, pick up 17 (18, 19, 20) loops along FRONT and BACK piece shoulder edges.

Working in the same manner as established, knit until piece measures 5 (6, 7, 7)" [12.7 (15.2, 17.8, 17.8) cm] from shoulder edge.

Cut A; join B.

With B, continue knitting until piece measures 13 (14, 15, 15)" [33 (35.6, 38, 38) cm] from shoulder edge.

Next Row: Knit 2 stitches together across to end—half of stitches decreased.

For sizes/custom variations with an ODD number of stitches left ONLY:

Next Row: Knit 2 stitches together, knit to end—1 stitch decreased.

CUFF (*on an even number of stitches*)

Row 1: *Knit 1, purl 1; repeat from * to end.
Row 2: *Purl 1, knit 1; repeat from * to end.

Repeat Rows 1–2 until cuff measures 3" (7.6 cm).

Maintaining pattern stitch, bind off.

Repeat for second sleeve.

finishing

Using a long strand of A, seam up the sides.

Weave in ends.

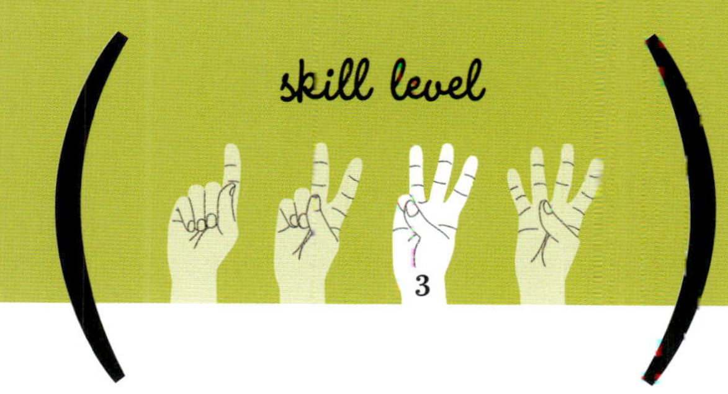

Crossover
cabled beanie

Calling all adventurous beginners! Who's ready to learn how to create cables? This hat is knit flat using a combination of knits and purls that create sections of stockinette and reverse stockinette stitches. The showstopper, though, is the center panel worked by cabling—cross two stitches over another two—every few rows. Get ready, the Crossover Cabled Beanie is a next-level project that will turn heads *and* warm them!

MATERIALS

- Super Bulky yarn (#6), 50% wool/50% acrylic (single ply), in one color
  Shown: K+C Cozy (7 oz/200 g, 87 yd/80 m, 50% superwash wool/45% premium acrylic/5% viscose): 1 skein
- Yarn needle with an extra-large eye

GAUGE

Approximately 4 stitches x 5 rows = 4" (10 cm) in stockinette stitch, DOUBLE STRANDED, slightly stretched.

SIZES

Unisex S/M (L/XL)

FINISHED MEASUREMENTS

20 (22)" [51 (56) cm] circumference
11" (28 cm) tall

notes

- This project is worked with a double strand of yarn, so if you're using only one (1) ball of yarn, you'll need to wind into TWO (2) evenly sized balls.

- This hat is made flat and from the top-down, then seamed up the back and gathered at the top for shaping. It's meant to have at least an inch (2.5 cm) of negative ease.

SPECIAL STITCH

Cable 4–Left: Skip first 2 stitches, letting the live loops carefully fall to the front of the work; knit next 2 stitches (taking care not to pull the yarn out of the previous loops); knit the 2 skipped loops. Cable made. (See page 17.)

Yarn Tip

Cascade Magnum yarn would work great for this project, too!

hat

Note: This project is worked with the right side facing you throughout. DO NOT TURN at the ends of rows.

Foundation Row: Chain 20 (22), or create a chain, using an even number of stitches, that's 1" (2.5 cm) shorter than desired circumference.

Note: If you're working with a different number of stitches than those listed, just be mindful of where the center 4 stitches of your piece are so you know where to place the cable, with the 3 purl stitches on each side.

Row 1: Working from right to left, pull up loop (stitch) in second chain, and every chain to end—20 (22) stitches (or desired number).
Row 2: Working from left to right, knit 5, purl 3, knit 4 (these will be your cable stitches), purl 3, knit 5.
Row 3: Working from right to left, knit 5, purl 3, knit 4 (these will be your cable stitches), purl 3, knit 5.
Row 4: Repeat Row 2.
Row 5: Knit 5, purl 3, Cable 4-Left, purl 3, knit 5.
Rows 6–9: Repeat Rows 2–5.
Rows 10–11: Repeat Row 2.

BRIM

Row 12: *Knit 1, purl 1; repeat from * to end.
Row 13: *Purl 1, knit 1; repeat from * to end.

Rib stitch established.

Bind off in rib stitch, leaving a long tail for seaming.

finishing

Seam back: Using the long tail and yarn needle, seam the sides of the piece together to create a tube.

Close top: With yarn needle and yarn tail, insert through center front and back (joining bound-off edge at center); make a stitch. Pinch side edges to same center point and stitch through both thicknesses. The top of the beanie will now be in an "x" formation.

Continue in this manner, pinching the opposite edges, and stitch them together until top of hat is completely closed.

Feed tail through top of hat to wrong side.

Weave in ends.

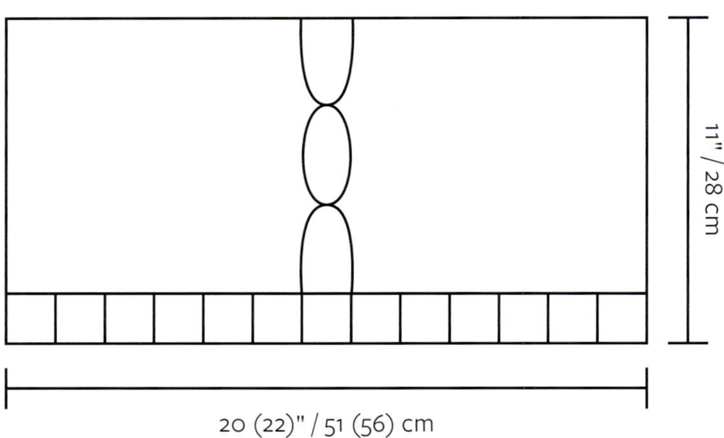

For a video tutorial on how to seam a hat or beanie top, scan the QR code.

Basket Case

basketweave cowl

Checkered meets textured thanks to a combination of knit and purl stitches. Paired with lush yarn, this basketweave stitch packs a lot of pattern punch. I love a project that looks impressive but isn't difficult to achieve. This one fits the bill. Bookmark the Basket Case cowl because all of your friends are going to want one!

MATERIALS

- Super Bulky yarn (#6), 100% wool (single ply), in one color
  Shown: Cascade Magnum (8.8 oz/250 g, 123 yd/112.5 m, 100% Peruvian highland wool): 1 hank
- Yarn needle with an extra-large eye

GAUGE

Approximately 4 stitches x 5 rows = 4" (10 cm) in basketweave pattern, using 2 strands of yarn held together (DOUBLE STRAND).

SIZE

One size

FINISHED MEASUREMENTS

28" (71 cm) circumference
10" (25 cm) wide

notes

- This project is worked with 2 strands of yarn held together throughout (DOUBLE STRANDED).
- If you're using the recommended yarn, you'll need to wind the hank into TWO (2) evenly sized balls.
- Project is worked with the right side facing you throughout. DO NOT TURN at the ends of rows.

cowl

Foundation Row: With DOUBLE STRAND of yarn, chain 28.

Row 1: Working from right to left, pull up loop (stitch) in second chain, and every chain to end. Do not turn—28 stitches.

Row 2: Working from left to right, *knit 2, purl 2; repeat from * to end of row.

Row 3: Working from right to left, *purl 2, knit 2; repeat from * to end of row.

Row 4: Working from left to right, *purl 2, knit 2; repeat from * to end of row.

Row 5: Working from right to left, *knit 2, purl 2; repeat from * to end of row.

Basketweave pattern established.

Repeat Rows 2–5 until piece measures 10" (25 cm) tall.

Bind off, leaving a long tail for seaming.

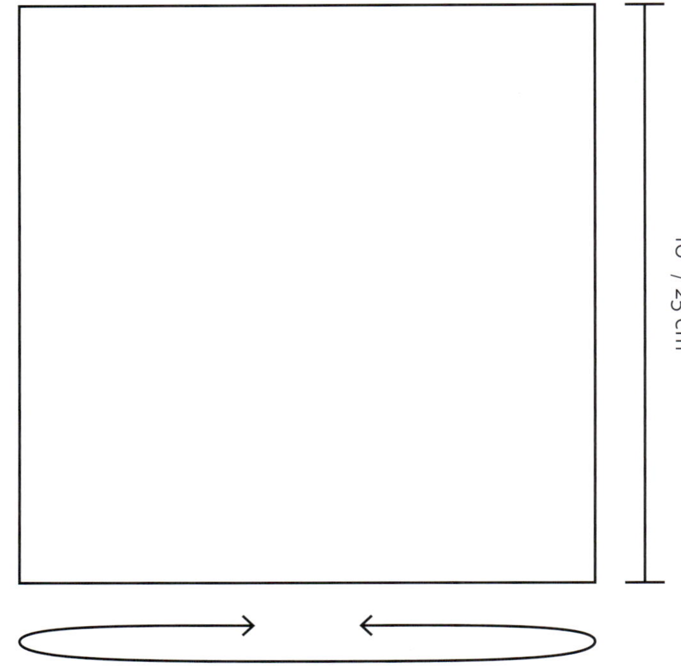

finishing

Using yarn needle and tail, sew the two short ends of the piece together to form cowl.

Flat Hatly

two-square beanie

Hand knitter, meet your first hat project! This cubic cutie is made by seaming two mostly knit-stitch squares (with just a dash of rib stitch) together, creating a hat shape. Make this project even simpler by going with a solid color instead of stripes. Either way, your happy head will thank you for it!

MATERIALS

- Bulky yarn (#5), 100% wool (double ply), in two colors
  Shown: Amano Yana XL (7.1 oz/200 g, 54 yd/50 m, 100% Peruvian highland wool): 1 hank each of Pink Bomb (A) and Estrella (B)
- Yarn needle with an extra-large eye

GAUGE

Approximately 4 stitches x 5 rows = 4" (10 cm) in stockinette stitch, with a ribbed band.

SIZES

S/M (L/XL)

FINISHED MEASUREMENTS

20 (22)" [51 (56) cm] circumference
Stretches to fit up to 21 (23)" [53 (58) cm] head.

notes

- Carry colors up along the side of work as you go.
- This project is worked with the right side facing you throughout. DO NOT TURN at the ends of rows.

front

Foundation Row: With A, ch 10 (12) (or make a 10 (12)" [25.5 (30.5) cm] chain).
Row 1: With A, and working from right to left, pull up loop (stitch) in second chain, and every chain to end. Do not turn throughout—10 (12) stitches (or desired number for 10 (12)" [25 (30.5) cm]).

Join B.

Row 2: With B, working from left to right, knit every stitch to end of row.
Row 3: With A, working from left to right, knit every stitch to end of row.
Row 4: With B, working from right to left, knit every stitch to end of row.
Row 5: With A, working from right to left, knit every stitch to end of row.

Repeat Rows 2–5 until piece measures 8" (20.5 cm).

Cut B.

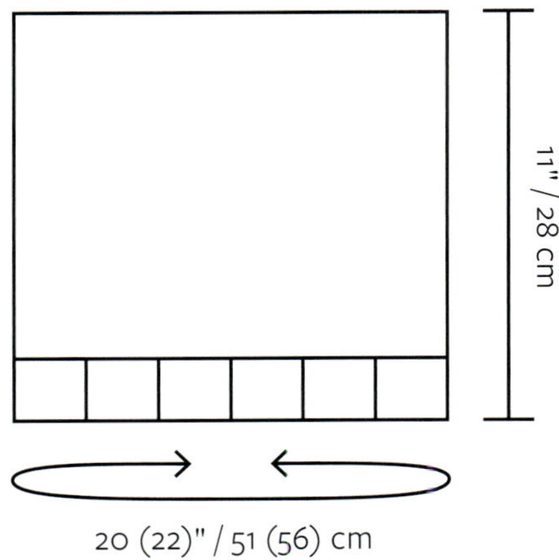

BRIM

Row 1: With A, working from left to right, *knit 1, purl 1; repeat from * to end of row.
Row 2: With A, working from right to left, *purl 1, knit 1; repeat from * to end of row.
Rows 3–4: Repeat Rows 1–2.

Bind off, leaving long tail for seaming.

back

Make same as for front.

finishing

Using a yarn needle (or fingers) and tails, seam up sides.

Weave in ends.

Measure Up!

When measuring your in-progress project, start at the foundation row edge, and stop at the row before the "live" loops. If it helps, think of those not-yet-knit loops as the "Os" reminding you, "Nooooo, don't measure us!"

Meta Tartan

plaid mega scarf

This extra-wide, super-smooshy scarf looks difficult to make but is actually a great project for beginners. The basic background is created by repeating the same two rows until you get the desired length. From there, your scarf canvas gets a glow-up with some woven-in stripes of contrasting colors of yarn.

MATERIALS

- Super Bulky yarn (#6), 50% wool/50% acrylic (single ply), in four colors
  Shown: Berroco Macro (8.75 oz/250 g, 112 yd/102 m, 50% wool/40% acrylic/10% alpaca): 2 hanks 6707 Beluga (A), approximately 14 yd/13 m 6746 Puffin Beak (B), and 10 yd/9 m each of 6715 Polar Night (C) and 6744 Snowy Owl Eyes (D)
- Yarn needle with an extra-large eye

GAUGE

Approximately 4 stitches x 8 rows = 4" (10 cm) in garter stitch, using 2 strands of yarn held together (DOUBLE STRAND).

FINISHED MEASUREMENTS

10" (25 cm) wide
65" (165 cm) long, excluding fringe

Fun Fact

In traditional knitting (with needles) when working on a flat piece of knitting, garter stitch is created by simply knitting every right side row and every wrong side row. With hand knitting, however, we're never working on the back of the piece, so the stitch construction needs to be different to create the same look.

notes

- This project is worked with 2 strands of yarn held together throughout (DOUBLE STRANDED).
- The project is worked with the right side facing you throughout. DO NOT TURN at the ends of rows.

SPECIAL STITCH

Garter Stitch: Knit 1 row from one side to the other; purl 1 row back in opposite direction.

KEY

- Beluga (A)
- Puffin Beak (B)
- Polar Night (C)
- Snowy Owl Eyes (D)

For a video tutorial on how to create woven plaid, scan the QR code.

scarf

Foundation Row: With 2 strands of A held together (DOUBLE STRANDED), loosely chain 9 [or make a 10" (25 cm)] chain.

Row 1: Working from right to left, pull up loop (stitch) in second chain, and every chain to end. Do not turn throughout—9 stitches [or desired number for 10" (25 cm)].

Row 2: Working from left to right, purl every stitch to end of row.

Row 3: Working from right to left, knit every stitch to end of row.

Row 4: Working from left to right, purl every stitch to end of row.

Repeat Rows 3–4 until piece measures 65" (165 cm).

Bind off.

finishing

CREATE "PLAID"

Note: For this step, you can use a yarn needle with an extra-large eye or your fingers.

Cut two 82" (208 cm) strands of B.

Holding 2 strands together (DOUBLE STRANDED), using graphic as a guide, and leaving a 5" (12.5 cm) tail for fringe, begin creating vertical stripes as follows:

- Starting at the lower right corner of one end, weave yarn over and under garter stitch bumps to opposite end. Turn, and weave back parallel to first stripe and to end. Leave remaining yarn as fringe.

- From here, you'll only be doing 1-row stripes. Following graphic, or doing your own thing, create additional woven stripes in colors B, C, and D.

Weave in nonfringe ends.

Groove Interrupted
THE HELP
BLINCOE
BETHLEHEM

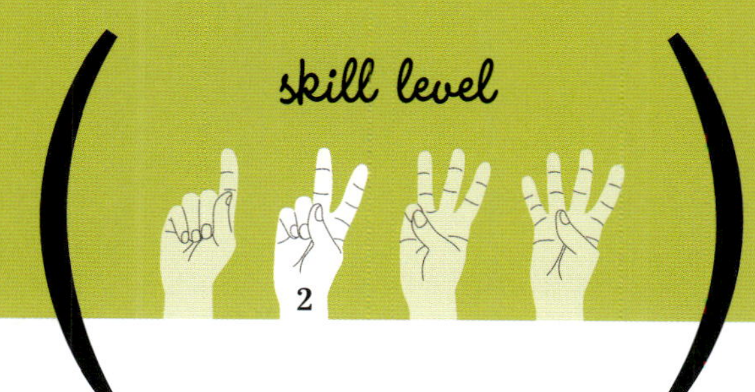

Pickpocket

marled pocket scarf

Everything's better with pockets, including accessories. This extra-wide scarf does double duty as the warmest neckwear on the block while being hand-inclusive (frozen fingers will be "out of pocket" with this project!). Our version plays with two types of color work—big, bold stripes that give "color blocking" vibes and marled stranding (don't worry, it sounds fancier than it is) for a fun twist.

MATERIALS

- Super Bulky yarn (#6), 100% wool (single ply), in two colors
  Shown: Wool & the Gang Crazy Sexy Wool (7.1 oz/200 g, 87 yd/80 m, 100% wool): 3 balls Lilac Powder (A) and 1 ball Chalk Yellow (B)
- Yarn needle with an extra-large eye

GAUGE

Approximately 4 stitches x 5 rows = 4" (10 cm) in stockinette stitch, using 2 strands of yarn held together (DOUBLE STRAND).

SIZE

One size

FINISHED MEASUREMENTS

11" (28 cm) wide
60" (152 cm) long

notes

- Marled sections are created by knitting with 1 strand each of colors A and B, held together. This forms a new color referred to as A/B.
- This project is worked with 2 strands of yarn held together throughout (DOUBLE STRANDED).
- The project is worked with the right side facing you throughout. DO NOT TURN at the ends of rows.

scarf

Foundation Row: With 2 strands of A held together, chain 11 [or make 11" (28 cm) chain].
Row 1: With A and working from right to left, pull up loop (stitch) in second chain, and every chain to end. Do not turn—11 stitches [or desired number for 11" (28 cm)].
Row 2: Working from left to right, purl every stitch to end of row.
Row 3: Working from right to left, purl 2, knit to last two stitches, purl 2.
Row 4: Working from left to right, purl 2, knit to last two stitches, purl 2.
Rows 5–18: Repeat Rows 3–4.

Cut A; join A/B.

Rows 19–35: With A/B, repeat Rows 3–18.

Changing colors, repeat Rows 3–35, once more.

With 2 strands of A only, repeat Rows 3–18 once more.

Last Row: Purl.

Bind off.

pockets (make 2)

Note: Carry color not in use up the side of the pocket while you work.

Foundation Row: With DOUBLE STRAND of A, chain 8 [or make an 8" (20.5 cm) chain].
Row 1: With A and working from right to left, pull up loop (stitch) in second chain, and every chain to end. Do not turn—8 stitches [or desired number for 8" (20 cm)].
Row 2: Working from left to right, knit every stitch to end of row.

Join B.

Row 3: With B, working from right to left, knit every stitch to end of row.
Row 4: With B, working from left to right, knit every stitch to end of row.
Row 5: With A, working from right to left, knit every stitch to end of row.
Row 6: With A, working from left to right, knit every stitch to end of row
Rows 7–10: Repeat Rows 3–6.

Cut A.

Row 11: With B, working from right to left, knit every stitch to end of row.
Row 12: Working from left to right, purl.

Bind off.

finishing

- Weave in ends.
- With a yarn needle and a SINGLE strand of A, and placing about 2" (5 cm) above scarf edge, sew pocket's sides and bottom to scarf. Repeat for other pocket on opposite end.
- Block piece, if necessary.

What Is "Marled"?

Marled yarn is often created by twisting two strands of different-colored yarn together before plying. The DIY version can be created by holding two strands of contrasting colored yarn together and knitting with them as if they were one.

POCKET
60" / 152 cm
7" / 18 cm
POCKET
7" / 18 cm
11" / 28 cm

Tee Tote-ler

T-shirt yarn tote bag

Ready to be a meta-maker? For this project, you'll not only make the bag but also the yarn to knit it. This colorful tote is created from upcycled T-shirts, so hit the thrift store, nab a bunch of oversize tees, and get creating your new favorite carryall!

MATERIALS

- 11–13 L–XXL thrifted T-shirts, in desired color palette
- Rotary cutter
- Self-healing mat
- Straightedge
- Scissors
- Bag handles
- Embroidery floss and embroidery needle

GAUGE

Approximately 3.75 stitches x 4.75 rows = 4" (10 cm) in stockinette stitch.

FINISHED MEASUREMENTS

24" (61 cm) circumference
15" (38 cm) tall, excluding handles

note

This bag is knit in the round, then seamed at the bottom.

How to Make Super-Bulky T-shirt Yarn—Basic Method

1. Gather T-shirts (the bigger the shirt, the better).
2. Cut off sleeves and lay T-shirts flat horizontally.
3. Using a rotary cutter (recommended) or scissors, cut T-shirts into 3" (8 cm) strips (they don't need to be perfect).
4. Stretch the strip out so that the edges curl in.
5. Tie strip ends to each other with knots; snip tied ends to approximately ½" (1.25 cm).
6. Roll T-shirt "yarn" into ball.

For a more advanced method of making T-shirt yarn, scan the QR code.

tote

Foundation Row: Leaving a 24" (61 cm) tail for seaming, chain 30.

Taking care not to twist the strip, join row to create a round by bringing your first and last stitches to meet; pull up loop from working yarn through last stitch.

From here, you'll be working in the round, so rotate the piece as necessary.

Round 1: Pull up a loop in the next 29 chain stitches—30 stitches. Place a marker to mark end of round.
Round 2: Knit every stitch to end of round.

Repeat Round 2 until piece measure 14" (35.5 cm).

Last Round: Purl every stitch to end of round.

Bind off.

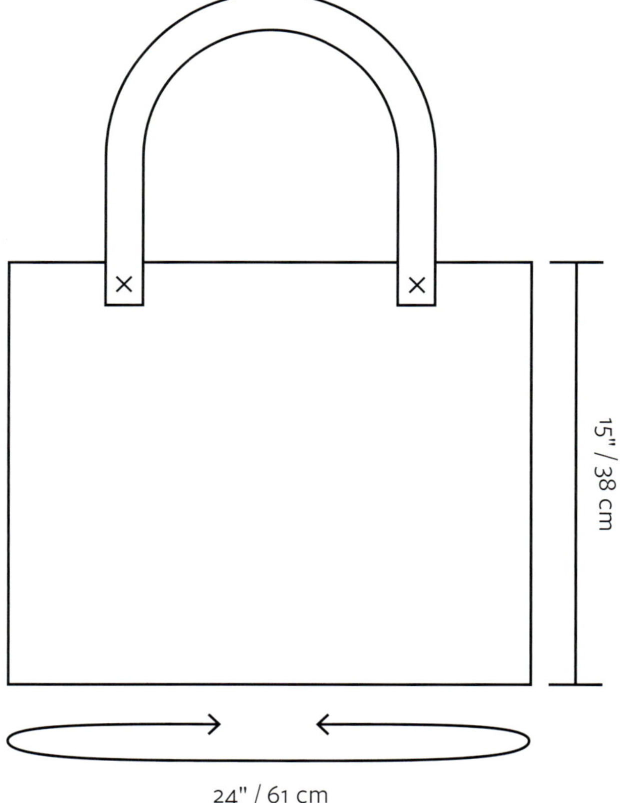

finishing

Using the tail, fingers, and either mattress stitch or whipstitch, sew the bottom of the bag closed.

Weave in ends.

ATTACH HANDLES

Using an embroidery needle and embroidery floss, securely hand sew straps to the bag.

Pro Tip

1. Make your own handles by cutting two 1" × 20" (2.5 x 51 cm) strips of faux leather, and two 1½" x 2" (4 x 5 cm) reinforcement pieces.
2. Using a leather punch, or awl, create four matching holes in all pieces. With straps on front and reinforcement pieces on the back, sew onto tote!

Fringe-fest

open-weave triangle shawl

Whether you're strolling along a beach, cozying up with some tea, or dancing at a music festival, a free-spirited (and be-fringed) shawl is a must-make. Knit from the top-center out, with thinner yarn for an open-weave, the Fringe-fest wrap is where it's at!

MATERIALS

- Super Bulky yarn (#6), 100% wool (thick and thin), in one color
  Shown: Knit Collage Spun Cloud (7.1 oz/200 g, 100 yd/91 m, 100% wool): 2 hanks Evergreen
- Removable stitch marker

GAUGE

Approximately 2.5 stitches x 3.75 rows = 4" (10 cm)

FINISHED MEASUREMENTS

78" (198 cm) at widest point
36" (91 cm) deep, excluding fringe

note

This project is made from the top center outward.

SPECIAL STITCH

Make 1 (increase): Lift the strand between the stitch you just worked and the next stitch, so you're holding it like a loop, and knit it as if it were a loop. Stitch made. (See page 28 of Stitch Tutorial section for tutorial.)

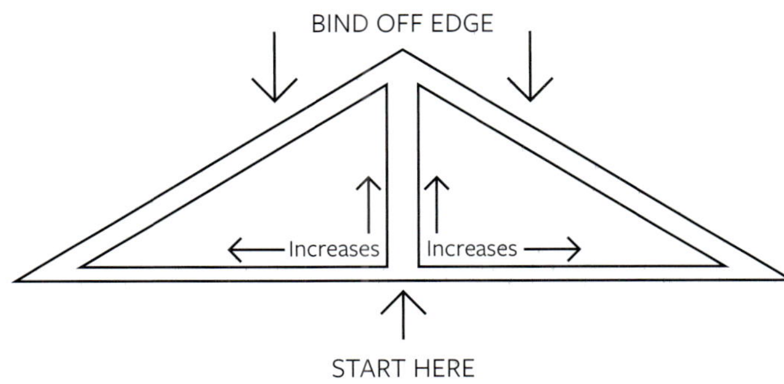

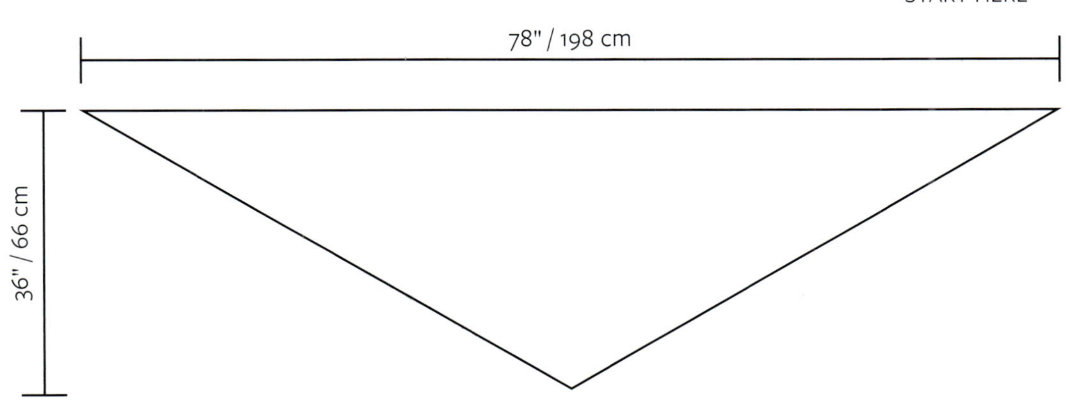

shawl

Foundation Row: Chain 5.

Row 1: Working from right to left, pick up a loop (stitch) in the 2nd stitch and every stitch to end—5 stitches.

Row 2: Working from left to right, knit every stitch to end of row.

Row 3: Working from right to left, [knit 1, make 1] TWICE, knit 1, place marker on that stitch (center), [make 1, knit 1] TWICE—7 stitches.

Row 4: Working from left to right, knit every stitch to end of row.

Row 5: Working from right to left, knit 1, make 1, knit to stitch before marker, make 1, remove marker, knit 1, replace marker on this stitch, make 1, knit to last stitch, make 1, knit 1—11 stitches.

Row 6: Working from left to right, knit every stitch to end of row.

Repeat Rows 5–6 ten times more—51 stitches.

Repeat Row 5 once more—55 stitches.

Last Row: Working from left to right, purl every stitch to end of row.

Bind off loosely.

Weave in ends.

Fringe

- Cut 34 strands of yarn each 18" (47 cm) long.
- Holding 2 strands of yarn together at a time and following the illustration at right, attach 17 pieces of fringe evenly across the lower edge of the shawl. Fold strands in half.
- With the right side facing, push the folded end of the strands through a stitch so that you see a loop on the wrong side of the project.
- Bring the created loop toward the front of your work and feed the ends of the strands through the loop.
- Make sure the fringe is taut against the shawl edge.

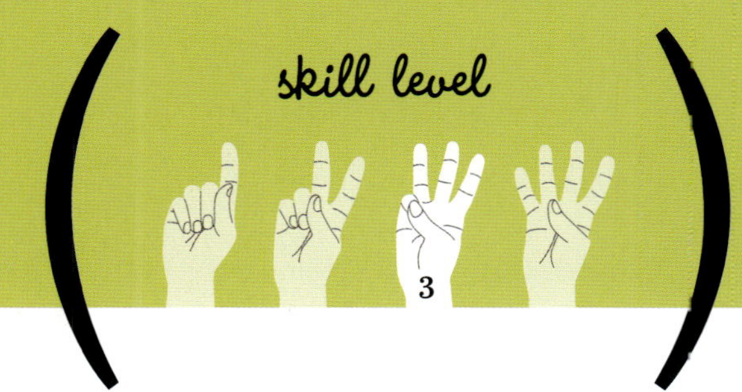

Bed. Coat.

ridiculously cuddly robe

This glorious bathrobe beast is basically a blanket with sleeves. Knit with Jumbo chenille yarn, it's as fluffy as it is fun to make. Looking for a wearable cloud? The search is over!

MATERIALS

- Jumbo yarn (#7), 100% polyester (chenille), in one color
  Shown: Bernat Blanket Big (10.5 oz/300 g, 32 yd/29 m, 100% polyester): 9 balls Green Splash
- Yarn needle with an extra-large eye

GAUGE

Approximately 2 stitches x 2.5 rows = 4" (10 cm) in stockinette stitch.

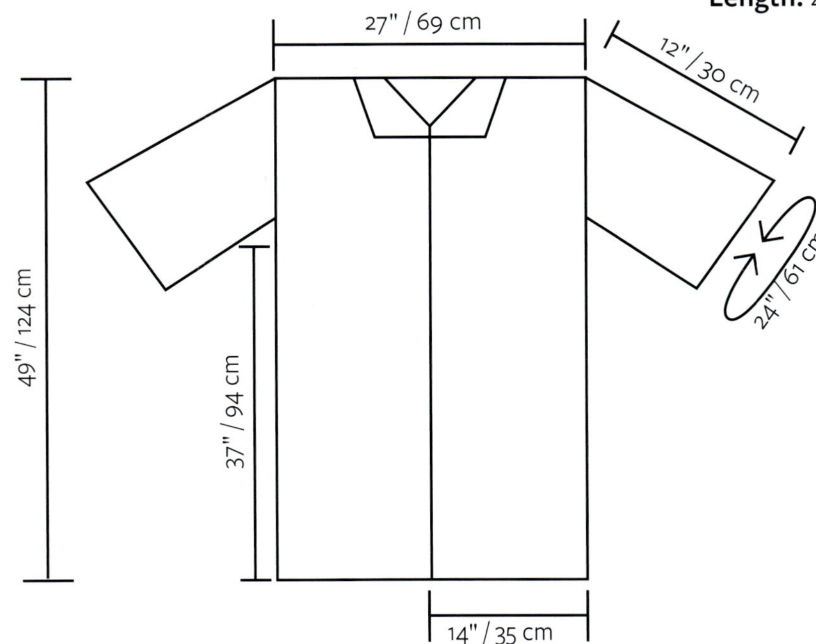

SIZE

One size. This robe is as much blanket as it is anything else, so due to the simple construction of this robe, the sizing is customizable. If you would like something smaller or larger, simply add or subtract stitches to your foundation chain for width, and knit more rows for length! Need a point of reference? Measure your favorite store-bought robe!

FINISHED MEASUREMENTS

Width: 27" (69 cm)
Length: 49" (124 cm)

back

Foundation Row: Chain 14 (or number needed for desired width of BACK).
Row 1: Pick up a loop in the 2nd chain, and every chain to end—14 stitches (or number to achieve desired width).
Row 2: Working from left to right, knit every stitch to end of row.
Row 3: Working from right to left, knit every stitch to end of row.

Repeat Rows 2–3 until piece measures 49" (124 cm).

Bind off.

front (make 2)

Foundation Row: Chain 7 (or number needed for HALF of desired width of FRONT).
Row 1: Pick up a loop in the 2nd chain, and every chain to end—7 stitches (or number to achieve HALF of desired width).
Row 2: Working from left to right, knit every stitch to end of row.
Row 3: Working from right to left, knit every stitch to end of row.

Repeat Rows 2–3 until piece measures 49" (124 cm).

Bind off.

SEAM SHOULDERS

Using a strand of yarn, your fingers (or a yarn needle with an extra-large eye), and starting from outer edge, sew together first 5 stitches of one FRONT panel to the back panel. The remaining FRONT edge will be left to fold over at the neckline. Repeat for opposite FRONT piece.

sleeves

With right sides facing you, lay the seamed piece on a flat surface.

Row 1: Using the shoulder seam of one side as a center point, pick up 12 loops along the BACK and FRONT edges—12 stitches.
Row 2: Working from left to right, knit every stitch to end of row.
Row 3: Working from right to left, knit every stitch to end of row.

Repeat Rows 2–3 until piece measures 11" (28 cm).

Last Row: Purl every stitch to end of row.

Bind off.

Repeat on opposite side for second sleeve.

front bands

Row 1: Pick up loops evenly along FRONT side edge (approximately 1 stitch per row, but add or subtract to make fabric lie flat).

Bind off.

Repeat on opposite side.

finishing

Using a strand of yarn, your fingers (or a yarn needle with an extra-large eye), and mattress stitch, sew up sides.

Weave in ends.

MAKE BELT

Make a 70" (178 cm) chain. Fasten off.

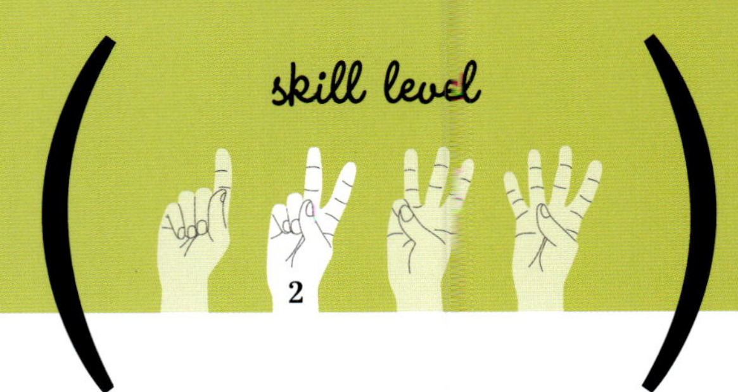

High Kicks

ribbed leg warmers

Calves meet coziness with these rib-stitched leg sleeves. Whether you're in a dance class or in your living room, the right music with these leg warmers will give you a case of the kicks!

MATERIALS

- Super Bulky yarn (#6), 100% wool (double ply), in one color
  Shown: Amano Yana XL (7.1 oz/200 g, 54 yd/50 m, 100% Peruvian highland wool): 2 hanks
- Stitch marker

GAUGE

Approximately 3.5 stitches x 3.5 rows = 4" (10 cm) in rib stitch.

SIZE

One size.

Note: The leg warmers can be made bigger by adding multiples of 2 stitches when creating the foundation row, and longer by continuing to knit until you're done!

FINISHED MEASUREMENTS

10" (25 cm) circumference
12" (30.5 cm) long

leg warmers (make 2)

Note: These leg warmers are worked in the round.

Foundation Row: Chain 12 (or an even number of stitches measuring your calf circumference plus 1" [2.5 cm]).
Row 1: Pull up a loop in every chain to end—12 stitches (or number for desired size).

Taking care not to twist the strip, join the row to create a round by bringing your first and last stitches to meet; pull up loop from working yarn through last stitch and place a marker for the beginning of the round.

From here, you'll work in rounds.

Round 2: *Knit 1, purl 1; repeat from * around.

Rib stitch established.

Repeat Round 2 until piece measures 12" (30.5 cm), or desired length.

While maintaining established rib stitch, bind off.

finishing

Weave in ends.

Twister

twisted headband/ear warmer

Clever seaming turns a simple, flat piece, created with finger-knit tubes, into this head-turning accessory. Cozy. Cute. Come on, let's make this!

MATERIALS

- Jumbo yarn (#7), 100% polyester (fuzzy), in one color.
  Shown: Lion Brand Go For Fleece Sherpa (6.5 oz/184 g, 89 yd/81 m, 100% polyester): 1 ball
- Yarn needle with an extra-large eye
- Scrap yarn

GAUGE

Not important for this project.

FINISHED MEASUREMENTS

Approximately 5" (12.5 cm) wide
Stretches to fit 21 (22, 23)" [53 (56, 58.5) cm] head circumference.

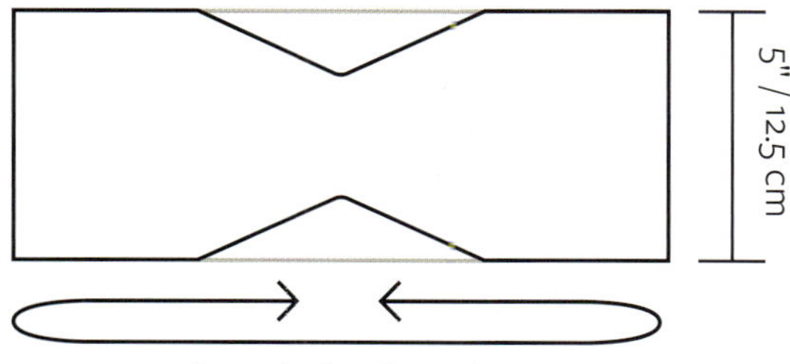

For a video tutorial on how to seam a twisted headband, scan the QR code.

band strips (make 2)

Weaving over 4 fingers, finger knit a 20 (21, 22)" [51 (53, 56) cm] piece, or piece that measures 1" (2.5 cm) shorter than head circumference.

Fasten off, leaving long tail for seaming.

finishing

Lay strips parallel on a flat surface.

Using tail and a yarn needle, sew the two pieces together to create one wide piece.

Using scrap yarn, with wrong sides facing out, fold each short end of headband in half, then interlock together in an "S" shape (see video in playlist for reference.) Using yarn tail, sew through all four layers.

Turn headband to right side with seam to inside.

Weave in ends.

Vest Is Best

mondo vest

East meets vest with this big and bold wardrobe popper! Think NYC fashion week piece meets attainable DIY staple. This top is made simply by knitting two hearty-sized rectangles, then seaming them up to the armholes. Cuffs are created by cleverly picking up loops and promptly binding them off. Sizing is customizable to whatever feels right for your body because *vest is best*!

MATERIALS

- Jumbo yarn (#7), 100% wool (roving), in one color
  Shown: Knit Collage Wanderlust (7.1 oz/200 g, 30 yd/27 m, 100% wool): 3 hanks Frolic
- A few yards finer-weight, smooth yarn for seaming
- Yarn needle with an extra-large eye
- Hand-sewing needle and coordinating thread for tacking ends in (optional)

GAUGE

Approximately 3.25 stitches x 4 rows = 4" (10 cm) in stockinette stitch.

SIZES

1 (2, 3, 4) customizable

FINISHED MEASUREMENTS

Length: 17 (17, 18, 18, 19)" [43 (43, 46, 46, 48) cm]
Bust: 30 (38, 46, 54)" [76 (96, 117, 122) cm]

notes

This vest is made up of 2 squares, which means it's totally customizable! If the measurements listed in this pattern don't work for you, simply measure the width of a garment that fits the way you like. From there, you'll just create a foundation chain that equals that measurement, and knit until it's the desired length.

- This vest can be worn with ease ranging from 2–6" (5–15 cm).

- This project is worked with the right side facing you throughout. DO NOT TURN at the ends of rows.

body (make 2)

Foundation Row: Chain 12 (15, 18, 21), or make a 15 (19, 23, 27)" [38 (48, 58, 68) cm] chain.
Row 1: Working from right to left, pull up loop (stitch) in second chain, and every chain to end. Do not turn—12 (15, 18, 21) stitches, or desired number.
Row 2: Working from left to right, knit every stitch to end of row.
Row 3: Working from right to left, knit every stitch to end of row.

Stockinette stitch established.

Continue as established, knitting every row until piece measures 16 (16, 17, 17, 18)" [40.5 (40.5, 43, 43, 46) cm] or 1" (2.5 cm) shorter than desired length.

Last 2 Rows: Purl.

Bind off.

finishing

With finer-weight yarn and yarn needle, sew shoulders to 4 (5,6 , 7)" [10 (13, 16.5, 18) cm] in from each edge.

Sew sides, leaving 10" (25 cm) open for armholes.

KNIT SLEEVE BANDS

Rejoining yarn, pick up a loop for every row.

Bind off.

Repeat for opposite side.

Weave in ends, tacking down with hand-sewing needle and thread when necessary.

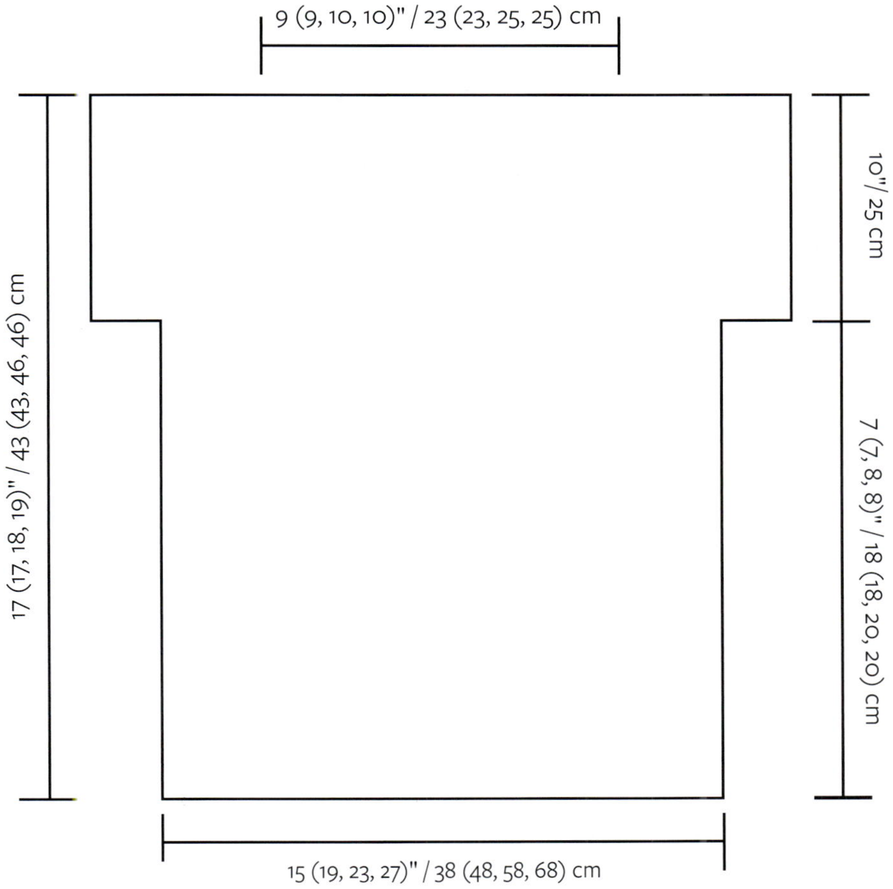

Pro Tip: Tack Down Ends

When working with extra-large yarns for making garments, the tails are often too bulky to weave in properly. To diminish the bulge, weave in ends for a shorter length, then tack them down with a hand-sewing needle and coordinating thread.

Chain-gling

velvety chain necklace

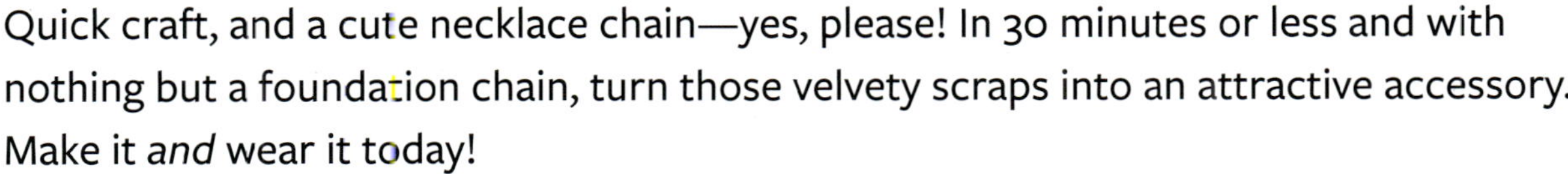

Quick craft, and a cute necklace chain—yes, please! In 30 minutes or less and with nothing but a foundation chain, turn those velvety scraps into an attractive accessory. Make it *and* wear it today!

MATERIALS

- Giant yarn (#8), 100% polyester (tube), in one color
  Shown: Lion Brand Cover Story Cozy Lux
  10.5 oz/300 g, 16 yd/15 m, 100% polyester)
- Hand-sewing needle and coordinating thread
- Two 30 mm jump rings
- Three 8 mm jump rings
- Lobster clasp
- Jewelry pliers

GAUGE

Approximately 2.5 stitches = 4" (10 cm) in foundation chain stitch.

FINISHED MEASUREMENTS

23" (58.5 cm) long, excluding jewelry findings.
This necklace sizing is customizable. Simply lengthen or shorten tails at both ends of the piece.

Fun Fact

The foundation chain stitch for hand knitting can also be called a finger-crocheted chain!

necklace

Leaving an 8" (20 cm) tail, chain 3.

Fasten off and make a simple knot butted up against the last chain (this will mirror the knot on the opposite end of your chain, created by the beginning slip knot).

Cut yarn, leaving an 8" (20 cm) tail.

finishing

ASSEMBLE NECKLACE

- Pull about 1" (2.5 cm) worth of stuff out of each end of the tube yarn.
- Thread an end through one larger jump ring and fold unstuffed end over it; fold fabric inside for a clean finish. Using sewing thread and hand-sewing needle, stitch end down to the underside of yarn tail; repeat for opposite end.
- Using jewelry pliers, manufacturers' instructions, and photo as a guide, attach smaller jump rings and lobster clasp.

Fur-bag

faux-fur cross-body purse

Function meets fashion with this plush purse. Knit with super-fluffy faux-fur yarn and layered with a canvas lining, this accessory combines simple sewing and no-needle knitting skills to result in a finished piece that's anything but basic.

Note: The actual knitting of this project is more of a level 1.5. It's working with the faux-fur yarn and the finishing that increases the difficulty level.

MATERIALS

- Super Bulky yarn (#6), 100% polyester (faux fur), in one color
  Shown: Knit Picks Fairy Tale Fur (3.5 oz/100 g, 71 yd/65 m,100% polyester): 2 balls Breccia
- Yarn needle with an extra-large eye
- ½ yard (0.5 m) canvas or barkcloth (for lining—with no wrong side, if possible)
- Scissors
- Hand-sewing needle and coordinating thread
- Sewing machine OR iron-on adhesive strips
- Magnetic snap or zipper
- Two D-rings
- Adjustable, cross-body bag strap (harvesting from a thrifted bag works great!)
- Sewing or binder

GAUGE

Approximately 5.25 stitches x 4.5 rows = 4" (10 cm) in stockinette stitch, using 2 strands of yarn held together (DOUBLE STRAND).

FINISHED MEASUREMENTS

14" (25.5 cm) wide
9" (23 cm) tall

note

This project is worked with 2 strands of yarn held together (DOUBLE STRANDED) throughout for purse body but is still very open-weaved. It's important to line it for the purse to be functional.

purse body (make 2)

Foundation Row: Chain 10.

Row 1: Working from left to right, pull up a stitch in the 2nd chain and every chain to end—10 stitches.

Row 2: Working from right to left, knit every stitch to end of row.

Row 3: Working from left to right, knit every stitch to end of row.

Row 4: Repeat Row 2.

Row 5: Working from left to right, knit 2 together–right, knit to last 2 stitches, knit 2 together–left—8 stitches.

Row 6: Repeat Row 2.

Row 7: Repeat Row 5—6 stitches.

Row 8: Repeat Row 2.

Bind off.

Sew Tack-y!

Faux-fur yarn can be a bit unwieldy, especially double stranded as for this project. Inevitably, there will be a dropped loop or one strand of the double strand that's slightly looser than the other. Fortunately, the fuzziness of the yarn can hide a whole lot.

A quick fix: Any offending loops can be woven in, then tacked down with a hand-sewing needle and thread.

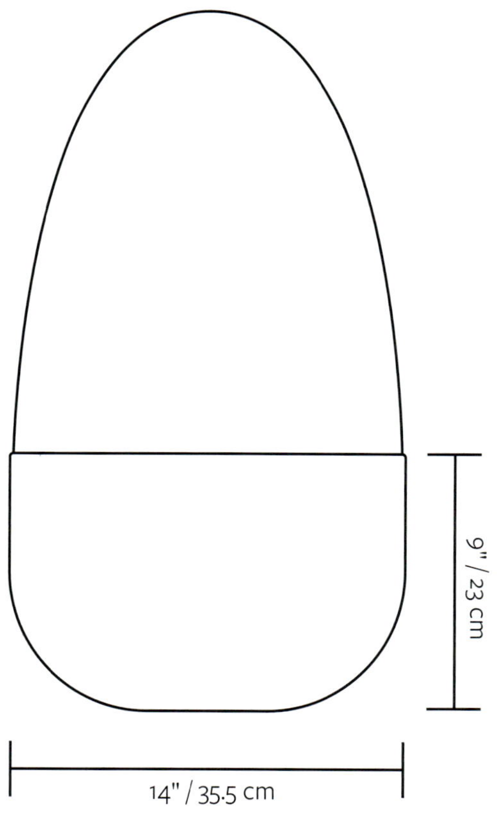

finishing

With wrong sides of purse facing out, using a single strand of yarn and yarn needle, whipstitch sides and bottom of bag together.

Weave in ends. Turn right sides out.

LINING

Note: The below instructions are for a basic lining with snap. For an elevated version, with a zipper and both inner and outer linings (the lighter, slightly visible through netting of stitches), see the Resources page at the end of this book.

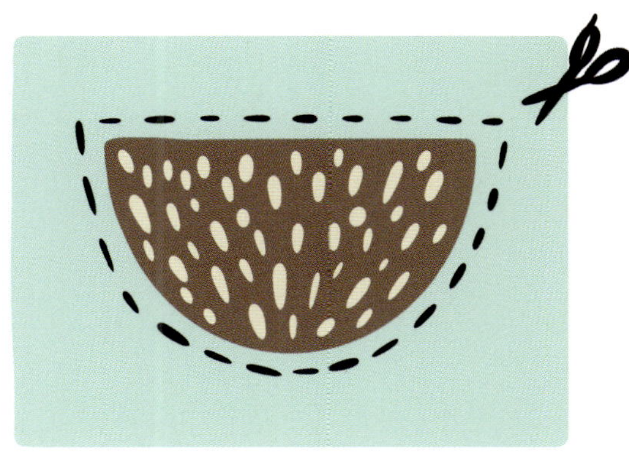

- Lay purse on top of a double layer of fabric. Trace a line ½" (2 cm) away from your purse, all the way around.
- Cut out fabric pieces.
- With wrong sides facing out, and using ½" (2 cm) seam allowance, machine sew, hand sew, or use iron-on adhesive to seam sides and bottom of pieces together.
- Fold top hem down ½" (2 cm) and press.
- Following manufacturers' instructions, attach magnetic button to the insides (this will be the right sides of the fabric) of lining.
- Insert lining into purse; hold in place with clips.
- Using hand-sewing needle, thread, and desired stitch (I like the invisible stitch), hand sew hem side of lining to inside of bag.

HANDLE

Using a large-eyed yarn needle and a single strand of yarn, whip stitch around the hardware ring of the strap and the top side of bag until strap is secure. Repeat for opposite side.

Feeling Fabric-phobic?

Looking for a fabric-free lining option? Try plastic canvas in a coordinating color! Simply cut two pieces the same size and shape as your purse body. Before you seam the purse front and backs together, using a yarn needle and a smooth, clean yarn, whipstitch plastic canvas to the wrong sides of each piece. Sew the bag together and voilà, you've added the necessary body to your bag!

One Skeiner

corded scarf

Cold neck? Quick, let's get cozy! Thanks to the scale of the chosen yarn, One Skeiner is made lickety-split requiring only ONE row of actual knitting. Embellish it with optional pom-poms, and in less than an hour, you'll have a statement scarf!

MATERIALS

- Giant yarn (#8), 100% polyester (tube), in one color
  Shown: Giant velvet yarn (2.2 lb/1 kg, 36 yd/33 m, 100% polyester)
- 2 faux-fur pom-poms (optional)
- Hand-sewing needle and coordinating thread

GAUGE

Approximately 10 stitches x 7 rows = 4" (10 cm) in knit stitch.

SIZE

One size

FINISHED MEASUREMENTS

3" (7.5 cm) wide
70" (179 cm) long

scarf

Foundation Row: Chain 42 (or number to create your desired-length scarf).

Row 1: Working from right to left, pull up loop (stitch) in second chain, and every chain to end. Do not turn—42 stitches (or number for desired length).

Bind off.

finishing

Using hand-sewing needle and thread, hand sew a pom-pom on each end of the scarf.

Weave in ends.

Space

projects for where you dwell

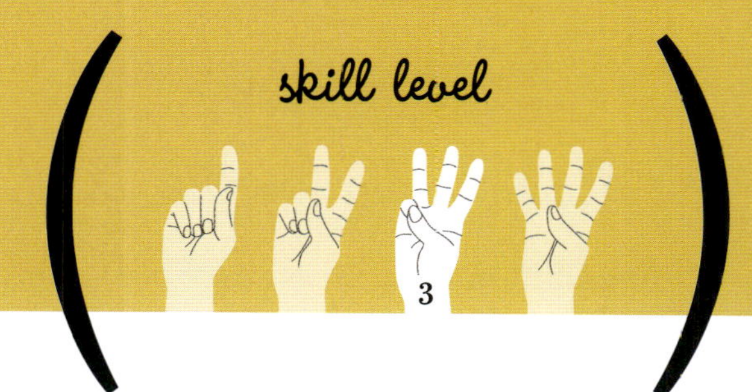

Petal Pusher

oversize flower pillow

A big ol' pillow adds comfy vibes to any room. Embellished with an optional, oversize flower, though? Well, that look gives pure cuteness!

MATERIALS

- Jumbo yarn (#7), 100% polyester (tube), in three colors
  Shown: Bernat Plush Big (8.8 oz/250 g, 45 yd/41 m, 100% polyester): 3 balls Off White (A) and 1 ball each of Leafy Green (B) and Caramel (C)
- Yarn needle with an extra-large eye
- 20" (51 cm) pillow form

GAUGE

Approximately 4 stitches x 3 rows = 4" (10 cm)

FINISHED MEASUREMENTS

20" (51 cm) square

FINGER CROCHET STITCHES

(Flower appliqué only)
See sidebar on page 85.

notes

Pillow Body

- This project is worked with the right side (smooth side) facing you throughout. DO NOT TURN at the ends of rows.

- For this project, the working yarn will always come from the back and be pulled through the loops to the front to create knit stitches. See page 26 of the Stitch Tutorials section for a tutorial.

Flower Petals

- These are finger crocheted. See stitch instructions on page 26.

pillow body (make 2)

Foundation Row: Chain 18 (or make a 20" [51 cm] chain).

Row 1: Working from right to left, and with smooth side facing, pull up a loop (stitch) in second chain, and every chain to end of row. Do not turn—18 stitches (or the number you need for a 20" (51 cm).

Row 2: Working from left to right, knit every stitch to end of row.

Row 3: Working from right to left, knit every stitch to end of row

Row 4: Working from left to right, knit every stitch to end of row.

Repeat Rows 3–4 until piece measures 20" (51 cm).

Bind off, leaving a long tail for seaming.

flower petals (make 5)

Note: These are finger crocheted. See stitch instructions on page 26.

Leaving a tail for sewing, chain 8 (length doesn't matter).

Row 1: Single crochet in 2nd chain from fingers, half double crochet in next chain, double crochet in next chain, triple crochet in next chain, double crochet in next chain, half-double crochet in next chain, single crochet in last chain; flip the piece over to work on the underside; single crochet into the bottom of the stitch you just worked, half double crochet in the next stitch, double crochet in the next stitch, triple crochet in the next stitch, double crochet in the next stitch, half double crochet in the next stitch, single crochet in the last stitch (bottom of where you began).

Fasten off.

finishing

EMBROIDER FLOWER CENTER

Using a yarn needle, a strand of B, and beginning at the center of the pillow front, embroider a French knot as follows:

1. Come up through a knit stitch in the fabric; wrap yarn around the needle twice.
2. Insert the needle tip into the fabric close to where you just came up. Push the wraps as close to the fabric as possible before slowly pulling the yarn through.

3. Repeat steps 1 and 2 to make a cluster of French knots for the flower center.

ATTACH FLOWER PETALS

Using Petal tails, yarn needle, and the photo as a guide, sew on each petal so they surround the flower center.

Weave in ends.

ASSEMBLE PILLOW

With right side facing out, use the long tail to sew three sides of the pillow pieces. Insert pillow form; sew remaining side.

KNIT APPLIED I-CORD PIPING

Note: You'll be attaching this to the outer perimeter of the pillow while you're knitting it.

Foundation Row: Chain 2.
Row 1: Working from right to left and with smooth side facing, pull up loop (stitch) in second chain. Do not turn—2 stitches.
Row 2: Working from right to left, knit each stitch.

Begin attaching piece to pillow as follows:

Row 3: Working from right to left, knit 1 stitch, then pair the 2nd stitch with a leg of a stitch right in front of the pillow seam (so you have 2 loops instead of 1), knit those two together as if they were one.

Pull the working yarn around the back of the work (this is what creates the cord look), repeat Row 3 (always working from right to left) for as long as it takes to knit, and attach cord piping all the way around the pillow.

Bind off. Join the piping end to the beginning to finish round by feeding the tail through the piece and stitching together.

Bury ends inside of pillow.

Flower Appliqué Finger Crochet Stitches

Single Crochet: With 1 loop from foundation chain already on your finger, insert finger through chain (or stitch) and pull up an additional loop (you'll now have 2 loops on your fingers); pull a working-yarn loop through BOTH loops on your fingers.

Half Double Crochet: With 1 loop from foundation chain already on your finger, wrap yarn around your fingers clockwise, insert finger through chain (or stitch), and pull up an additional loop (you'll now have 3 loops on your fingers, including the wrap); pull a working-yarn loop through ALL THREE loops on your fingers.

Double Crochet: With 1 loop from foundation chain already on your finger, wrap yarn around your fingers clockwise, insert finger through chain (or stitch), and pull up an additional loop (you'll now have 3 loops on your fingers, including the wrap); wrap yarn around your fingers clockwise and pull a working-yarn loop through TWO (2) loops on your fingers twice.

Triple Crochet: With 1 loop from foundation chain already on your finger, wrap yarn around your fingers clockwise TWICE, insert finger through chain (or stitch), and pull up an additional loop (you'll now have 4 loops on your fingers, including the wraps); wrap yarn around your fingers clockwise pull a working-yarn loop through TWO (2) loops on your fingers three times.

Scan the QR code for a video tutorial on crocheting the petals and knitting the applied i-cord.

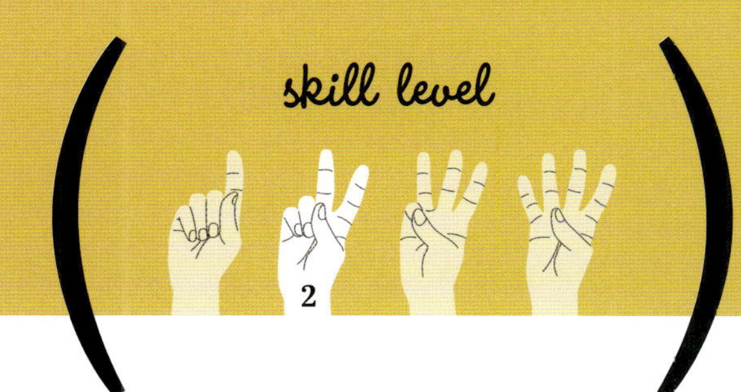

So Fluffy!

faux-fur throw

Add warmth to your room's decor with this simple and stylish faux-fur throw. Knit in basic stockinette stitch (knitting back and forth for every row) with a furry yarn, this blanket is a stunner of subterfuge stitches!

MATERIALS

- Super Bulky yarn (#6), 100% polyester (faux fur), in one color
  Shown: Loops & Thread Faux Fur (10.5 oz/297 g, 56 yd/51 m, 100% polyester): 6 Balls Husky

GAUGE

Approximately 2.5 stitches x 2.5 rows = 4" (10 cm).

FINISHED MEASUREMENTS

60" (152 cm)

note

This pattern will work with any number of yarn types. If you don't have access to faux-fur yarn, try chenille or roving yarns. Without the "fur" to fill the holes, though, you'll need to move up yarn weights to a Jumbo (#7) to avoid a net effect.

throw

Foundation Row: Chain 40 (or as many as it takes to get to desired width for a throw).

Row 1: Working from right to left, pull up a loop (stitch) in second chain and every chain to end. Do not turn here and throughout—40 stitches (or desired number).

Row 2: Working from left to right, knit every stitch to end of row.

Row 3: Working from right to left, knit every stitch to end of row.

Repeat Rows 2–3 until piece measures 60" (152 cm), or desired length.

Bind off.

Pro Tip

When working with furry yarns, individual stitches aren't as visible as they would be with a smoother kind, which makes it much easier to miss when you accidentally drop a stitch. Take time to count your stitches at the end of EVERY row. Trust me, it's worth the effort.

finishing

Weave in ends.

Rug Roomie

seed stitch mat

Behold, a tricoter (that's French for knitting) treat for your toes! Textured seed stitch paired with Jumbo chenille-style yarn come together in squishy goodness for a rug fit for your favorite room.

MATERIALS

- Jumbo yarn (#7), 100% polyester (chenille), in two colors
  Shown: Bernat Blanket Big (10.6 oz/300 g, 32 yd/29 m, 100% polyester): 2 balls Mottled Taupe (A) and 1 ball Black (B)
- No-slip rug pad (optional)

GAUGE

Approximately 2 stitches x 2.5 row = 4" (10 cm) in seed stitch.

FINISHED MEASUREMENTS

Approximately 34" x 40" (86 x 102 cm)

SPECIAL STITCH

Seed stitch: Alternating knit and purl stitches every stitch and row.

Seed Stitch: Read-y, Set, Know!

When working patterns that combine knits and purls, it's helpful to know how to read your stitches. A knit stitch looks like an upside-down raindrop, and a purl stitch looks like a little bump.

rug body

Foundation Row: With A, loosely chain 17 (or number needed to achieve desired width.)
Row 1: Working from right to left, pick up a loop (stitch) in the 2nd stitch and every stitch to end—17 stitches (or desired number).
Row 2: Working from left to right, *purl 1, knit 1; repeat from * to end of row.
Row 3: Working from right to left, *purl 1, knit 1; repeat from * to end of row.

Repeat Rows 2–3 until piece measures 28" (71 cm) or 6" (15 cm) less than desired length.

Bind off in pattern stitch (purl the knit stitches and knit the purl stitches as you bind them off).

border

Row 1: With B, pick up 11 stitches (or as many needed for an even edge) along one short end—11 stitches (or desired number).
Row 2: Working from left to right, knit every stitch to end of row.

Bind off.

Repeat for opposite end.

Repeat the process for both long sides, picking up 20 stitches (or necessary number for an even edge) evenly across rug edge and sides of short ends.

finishing

Weave in ends.

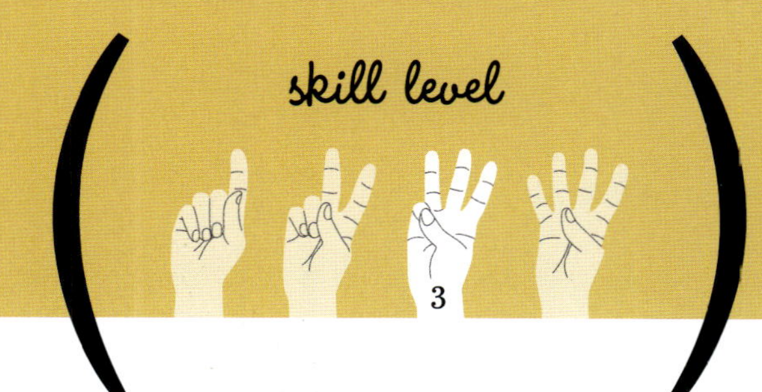

Shortcake

strawberry plushie

It's hard to resist an oversize plushie. When it's berry-licious like Shortcake, though, it's simply irresistible. Hand-knit with a double strand of chenille yarn and embellished with felt, this fantastical fruit forms in no time. Life is sweet—so is this project.

MATERIALS

- Jumbo yarn (#7), 100% polyester (chenille), in two colors
  Shown: Bernat Blanket Extra (10.5 oz/300 g, 97 yd/87 m, 100% Polyester): 1 ball each of Crimson (A) and Deep Sea (B)
- 1 sheet of yellow felt
- Hand-sewing needle and coordinating thread
- Scissors

GAUGE

Not important for this project.

FINISHED MEASUREMENTS

Approximately 15" (38 cm) tall x 24" (61 cm) around widest point, after stuffing.

notes

- This project is made with a hand-knit body and finger crochet stem. It's embellished with hand-sewn felt seeds.
- This project is worked with 2 strands of yarn held together (DOUBLE STRANDED).
- See page 26 of the Stitch Tutorials section for finger crochet tutorials.

SPECIAL STICHES

Single Crochet (finger crochet): With the loop from the last stitch worked still on your fingers, insert fingers in appropriate chain, pull up another loop (2 loops on fingers); pull yarn through BOTH loops. Single crochet stitch complete.

Picot Stitch (finger crochet): Work a single crochet stitch; chain 3 stitches; slip a stitch in the 3rd chain from your fingers. Picot stitch complete.

For a video tutorial of this project, scan the QR code.

berry

Foundation Row: With a DOUBLE strand of A, chain 18.
Row 1: Working from left to right, put up a stitch in the 2nd chain and every chain to end—18 stitches.
Row 2: Working from right to left, knit.
Row 3: Working from left to right, knit.

Repeat Rows 2–3 until piece measures 10" (25 cm).

Next Row: Working from right to left, knit 2 together–left, knit 6, knit 2 together–left, knit to last 2 stitches, knit 2 together–right—15 stitches.
Next Row: Repeat Row 3.
Last Row: Working from right to left, knit 1, *knit 2 together (direction doesn't matter); repeat from * to end—8 stitches.

Cut a long tail for seaming; thread tail through the live loops and cinch tight.

finishing

BERRY

- Using the tail, fingers, and mattress stitch, sew up the side. Do NOT cut tail.
- Stuff berry body with the remaining yarn left from the skein.
- Weave tail in and out of the stitches around the top of berry; pull to cinch.
- Sew shut.

Note: For a plumper plushie, you need a portion of an additional ball of A for stuffing.

SEEDS

- Scan and print out the full-size pattern (see below). Using the pattern, cut out 8 felt seeds.
- Using needle and thread, and photo as a guide, hand sew seeds to berry.

MAKE STEM

Foundation Row: With ONE (1) strand only of B, chain 21.
Row 1: Picot stitch in 2nd chain from fingers, single crochet in next chain, *picot stitch, single crochet in next chain; repeat from * to end of chain—20 stitches.

Fasten off, leaving a tail for attaching to berry.

Scrunch piece into stem shape. Using the tail and your fingers, sew stem to top of berry. Stuff tails inside.

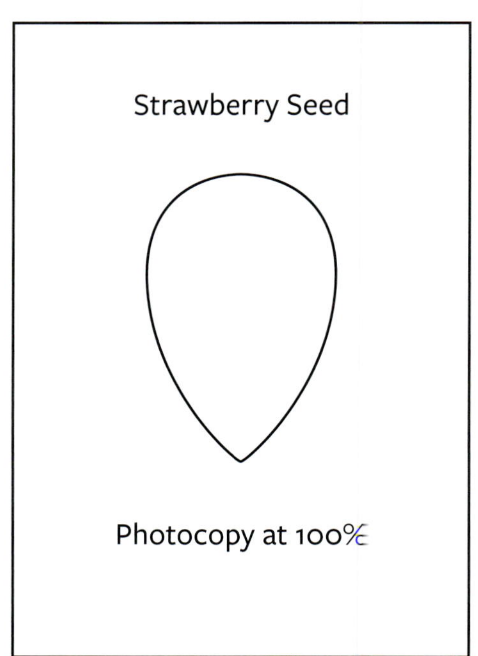

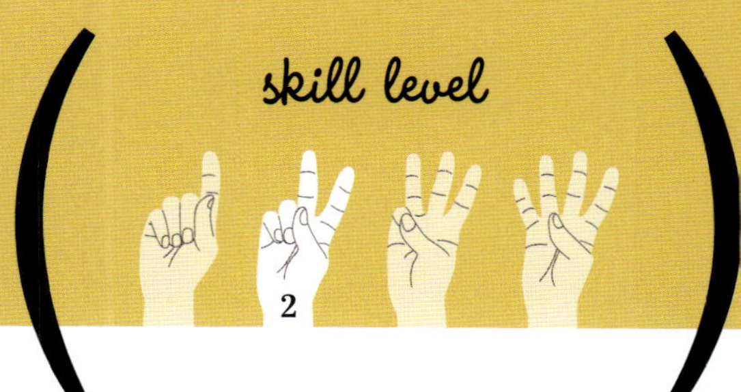

White Witch Wreath

finger-knit home decor

Whether winter is coming or spring has sprung, this wreath brings the warmth of yarn and a nod to nature into the home. Customize yours for any room or anyone!

MATERIALS

- Super Bulky yarn (#6), 100% polyester (chenille), in one color
  Shown: Loops & Threads Chenille Home Slim (8.8 oz/250 g, 218 yd/200 m, 100% polyester): 1 ball
- 15" (38 cm) foam wreath
- Glue gun
- Approximately 18" (46 cm) of 1" (2.5 cm)-wide ribbon (for hanger)
- Assorted faux foliage in coordinating palette
- Piece of 3" (7.5 cm)-wide ribbon
- Floral wire and cutter (optional)

GAUGE

Not important for this project.

FINISHED MEASUREMENTS

15" (38 cm) diameter

wreath

Yarn wrap over 3 fingers—3 stitches.

Finger knit piece until the ball of yarn is finished.

Loosely fasten off.

finishing

WRAPPING WREATH

- Weave in the beginning tail.
- Starting anywhere on the back of the wreath and using hot glue, secure the end of the piece to the foam.
- Wrap piece around the wreath several times and glue down to secure. Repeat this process until wreath is completely covered.
- If you have any knitting left, carefully unfasten the end and unravel unneeded portion Re-fasten off, cut end, tuck in, and glue down.

EMBELLISHING WREATH

- Arrange foliage, using photo as a guide, and attach to the wreath with hot glue or by tying on with floral wire.
- Cover center of foliage by wrapping wider ribbing around it and the wreath. Hot glue into place on the back.

ATTACH HANGER

Fold thinner ribbon in half and attach it to wreath top as if it were fringe (see illustration at right). Knit the two ends together toward the top. Trim to make even.

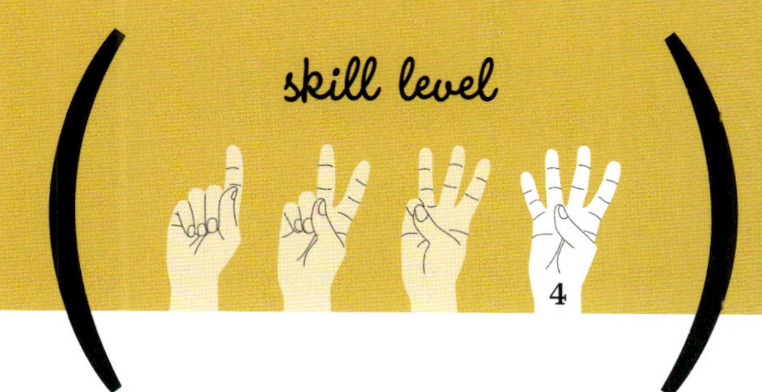

Building Block Blanket

log cabin throw

Playing with scale is one of the most visually gratifying ways to transform techniques and motifs from traditional to on-trend. This blanket is created using the Log Cabin method, historically knit at a MUCH smaller gauge and intended to duplicate an age-old quilt block. Supersize, though, this pattern is bold, graphic, and contemporary.

MATERIALS

- Jumbo yarn (#7), 100% polyester (tube), in five colors
  Shown: Bernat Plush Big (8.8 oz/250 g, 45 yd/41 m, 100% polyester): 5 balls Brick (A); 1 ball each of Brick Terra Multi (B), Carmel (C), and Elderberry (D); and 6 balls Off White (E)

GAUGE

Approximately 3.25 stitches x 6.5 rows = 4" (10 cm) in garter stitch.

FINISHED MEASUREMENTS

52" (132 cm) square

notes

- This project is made from the center-out by knitting a block, binding off stitches, rotating the piece 90 degrees, picking up stitches along that edge, then knitting the next block. Use the diagram for directional reference.
- This project is worked in garter stitch (knit 1 row, purl 1 row). For every 2 rows a bump will be created. When picking up stitches along the side of a block, you'll always pick up 1 stitch per garter bump. The unbound-off stitch from the block before counts as the first stitch, so skip the first bump.

Back Breaks

When working with Jumbo yarn on a mega-piece, be sure to take care of the bod. Take frequent breaks to stretch out that upper back.

Block 1

Foundation Row: With A, chain 8.
Row 1: Working from right to left, pick up a loop in the 2nd stitch and every stitch to end—8 stitches.
Row 2: Working from left to right, purl every stitch to end of row.
Row 3: Working from right to left, knit every stitch to end of row.
Row 4: Working from left to right, purl every stitch to end of row.
Rows 5–20: Repeat Rows 3–4.

Bind off 7 stitches—1 stitch remains.

Cut A; rotate piece 90 degrees to the right.

Block 2

Join B.

Row 1: With B, pick up 9 loops along the side of Block 1—10 stitches.
Row 2: Working from left to right, purl every stitch to end of row.
Row 3: Working from right to left, knit every stitch to end of row.
Row 4: Working from left to right, purl every stitch to end of row.
Rows 5–8: Repeat Rows 3–4.

Bind off 9 stitches—1 stitch remains.

Cut B; rotate piece 90 degrees to the right.

Block 3

Join C.

Row 1: With C, pick up 10 loops (3 along the side of Block 2, 8 along bottom of Block 1)—11 stitches.
Row 2: Working from left to right, purl every stitch to end of row.
Row 3: Working from right to left, knit every stitch to end of row.
Row 4: Working from left to right, purl every stitch to end of row.
Rows 5–10: Repeat Rows 3–4.

Bind off 10 stitches—1 stitch remains.

Cut C; rotate piece 90 degrees to the right.

Block 4

Join D.

Row 1: With D, pick up 14 loops (3 along the side of Block 3, 10 along the side of Block 1)—15 stitches.
Row 2: Working from left to right, purl every stitch to end of row.
Row 3: Working from right to left, knit every stitch to end of row.
Row 4: Working from left to right, purl every stitch to end of row.
Rows 5–8: Repeat Rows 3–4.

Bind off 14 stitches—1 stitch remains.

Cut D; rotate piece 90 degrees to the right.

Block 5

Join E.

Row 1: With E, pick up 15 loops (3 along side of Block 4, 8 along bottom of Block 1, 4 along side of Block 2)—16 stitches.
Rows 2–8: Work same as for Block 4.

Bind off 15 stitches—1 stitch remains.

Rotate piece 90 degrees to the right

block 6

Row 1: Pick up 18 loops (3 along the side of Block 5, 10 along top of Block 2, and 4 along the side of Block 3)—19 stitches.
Rows 2–8: Work same as for Block 4.

Bind off 18 stitches—1 stitch remains.

Rotate piece 90 degrees to the right.

block 7

Row 1: Pick up 19 loops (3 along the side of Block 6, 12 along top of Block 3, 4 along the side of Block 4)—20 stitches.
Rows 2–8: Work same as for Block 4.

Bind off 19 stitches—1 stitch remains.

Rotate piece 90 degrees to the right.

52" / 132 cm

52" / 132 cm

block 8

Row 1: Pick up 22 loops (3 along side of Block 7, 15 along top of Block 4, 4 along side of Block 5)—23 stitches.
Rows 2–8: Work same as for Block 4.

Bind off 22 stitches—1 stitch remains.

Rotate piece 90 degrees to the right.

blocks 9–12

Continue as established, picking up stitches evenly (see numbers below) along edges and knitting 8 rows, bind off to last stitch, and rotate.
Block 9 = 23 stitches.
Block 10 = 24 stitches.
Block 11 = 27 stitches.
Block 12 = 28 stitches.

Cut E.

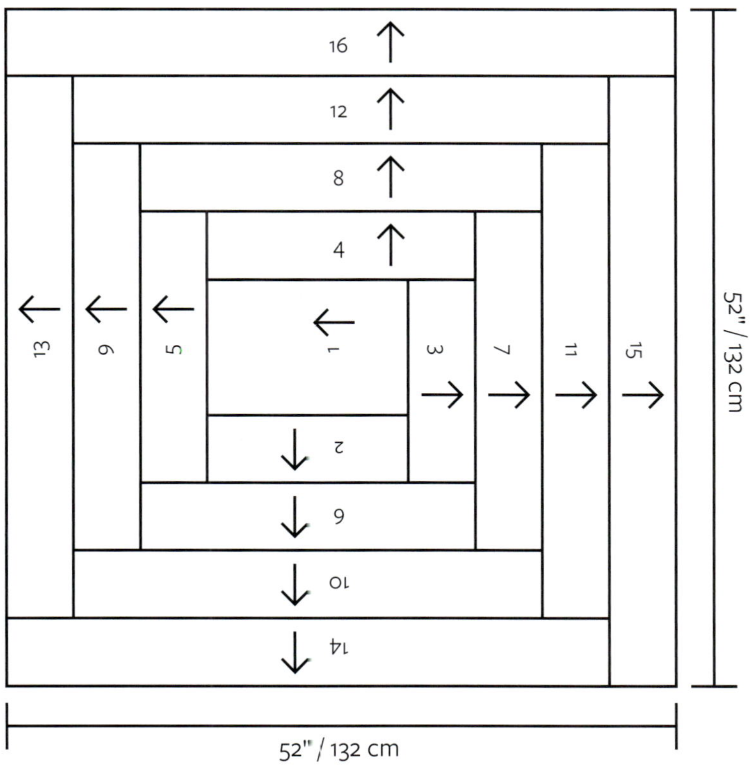

blocks 13–16

Join A.

With A, work same as for Blocks 9–12.
Block 13 = 31 stitches.
Block 14 = 32 stitches.
Block 15 = 33 stitches.
Block 16 = 37 stitches.

finishing

Weave in ends.

Posh Pallet

floor cushion

Giant velveteen yarn eads the luxury way in this project. Stockinette stitch shines as the main-stage techn que in this Posh Pallet. It's then elevated with whipstitching that cleverly mocks a corc ed finishing. Floor seating has never looked so chic!

MATERIALS

- Giant yarn (#8), 100% polyester (tube), in one color *Shown: Giant velvet tube yarn (2.2 lb/1 kg, 36 yd/33 m, 100% polyester): 5 balls*
- 24" x 24" x 4" (61 x 61 x 10 cm) upholstery foam
- Hand-sewing needle and coordinating thread
- Yarn clips, binder clips, or clothespins for assembling (optional)

GAUGE

Approximately 1.75 stitches x 2.25 rows = 4" (10 cm) in stockinette stitch.

FINISHED MEASUREMENTS

24" x 24" x 4" (61 x 61 x 10 cm)

front

Foundation Row: Loosely chain 11 (or number to make a 24" [61 cm] chain).
Row 1: Working from right to left, pick up a loop (stitch) in the 2nd stitch and every stitch to end—11 stitches (or number needed for length).
Row 2: Working from left to right, knit every stitch to end of row.
Row 3: Working from right to left, knit every stitch to end of row.

Repeat Rows 2–3 until piece measures 24" (61 cm).

Bind off.

back

Work same as for front.

sides strip

Foundation Row: Loosely chain 251 (or number to make a 96" [244 cm chain]).
Row 1: Working from right to left, pick up a loop (stitch) in the 2nd stitch and every stitch to end—251 stitches (or number needed for length).
Row 2: Working from left to right, knit every stitch to end of row.
Row 3: Working from right to left, knit every stitch to end of row.

Bind off leaving a VERY long (about 3 times the length of the piece, if possible) tail for seaming.

finishing

Avoid bulk from weaving in ends by cutting down tails to approximately 2" (5 cm). Pull enough stuffing from the inner tube of the yarn out of the tail to allow the velveteen outer fabric to be folded in for a clean edge. Tuck tail in the underside of piece, and using needle and thread, sew down the ends to securely attach it.

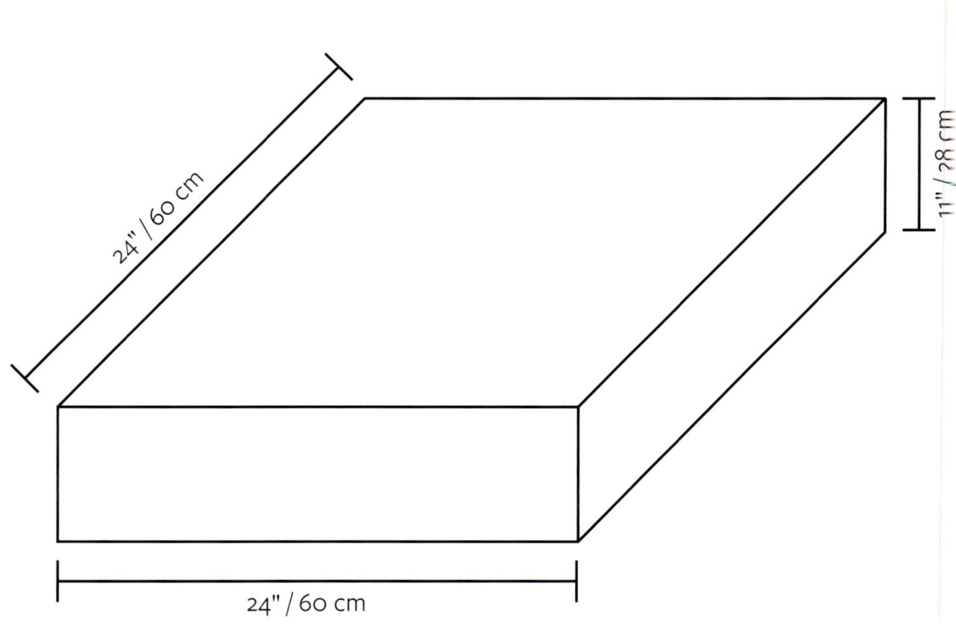

assembly

- Lay back piece on a flat surface.
- You'll now begin attaching the sides strip around the perimeter of the back. It's helpful to use clips here to hold the strip in place as you work. Please note, you may have to ease (stretch or squish) the strip to fit around all 4 sides of the back.
- Using the tail, whipstitch (see illustration at right) pieces together around all 4 sides of the back.
- Continuing with tail, but this time using mattress stitch (to create a less visible seam), sew short end of sides strip together to form the round.
- Place upholstery foam on top of back, nestled inside sides strip.
- Lay front piece on top of upholstery foam.
- Revert to whipstitch to attach front to sides strip.
- Snip and sew final end.

Whipstitch

Whipstitch, as the name implies, is a method of seaming that calls for coming up through both layers of fabric to be seamed, then "whipping" around the layers, coming up in the fabric where you'd like your next stitch. For this project, I recommend whipstitching around every loop (stitch) all the way around.

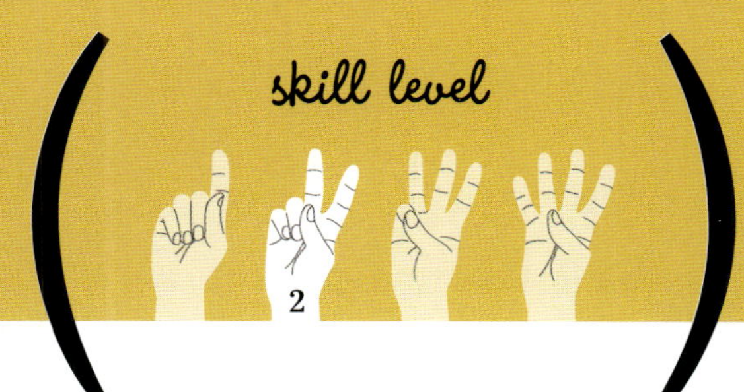

Cushy Life

squishy pet bed

Does your pet deserve a plush place to rest their weary head? Enter, the Cushy Life. Plump tube yarn, knitted up at an almost cartoony scale, results in a bed worthy of your bestest boys and girls!

MATERIALS

- Jumbo yarn (#7), 100% polyester (tube), in one color
  Shown: Lion Brand Cover Story Squish Stitch (19.4 oz/550 g, 26 yd/24 m, 100% polyester): 3 (4) balls Mallard or Chili Pepper
- Hand-sewing needle and coordinating thread

GAUGE

Approximately 2 stitches x 3.5 rows = 4" (10 cm) in stockinette stitch.

SIZE

Small (Large)

FINISHED MEASUREMENTS

Small: 15" x 16" x 8" (38 x 40.5 x 20 cm)
Large: 20" x 24" x 8" (51 x 61 x 20 cm)

base

Foundation Row: Chain 7.
Row 1: Working from right to left, pull up loop (stitch) in second chain, and every chain to end. Do not turn here and throughout—7 stitches.
Row 2: Working from left to right, knit 1, purl to last stitch, knit 1.
Row 3 (increase row): Working from right to left, knit 1, make 1, knit to last stitch, make 1, knit 1—9 stitches.
Row 4: Working from left to right, knit 1, purl to last stitch, knit 1.

Large only:
Rows 5–6: Repeat Rows 3 and 4—11 stitches.

All sizes:
Row 7: Working from right to left, knit.
Row 8: Working from left to right, knit 1, purl to last stitch, knit 1.

Repeat Rows 7–8 until piece measures 13 (21)" [33 (53) cm], ending with a Row 7.

Next Row (decrease row): Working from left to right, knit 1, knit 2 together–left (see page 19 of the Stitch Tutorials section), knit to last 3 stitches, knit 2 together–right, knit 1—7 (9) stitches.
Next Row: Working from right to left, knit 1, purl to last stitch, knit 1.

Large only:
Repeat last 2 rows.

All sizes:
Bind off, but do not cut yarn.

SIDES

Notes:

1. The loop left after binding off (bind-off loop) will count as 1 stitch.
2. When picking up stitches, pick up 1 for every garter stitch bump along the sides of rows, and 1 for every stitch along each short end.

Beginning at a short edge, pick up 27 (37) loops (see page 26 of the Stitch Tutorials section) around as follows:

Size small:
Counting bind-off loop as first stitch, pick up 6 more stitches along first short side, 7 stitches along first long side, 7 stitches along second short end, and 7 stitches along second long side—28 stitches.

Size large:
Counting bind-off loop as first stitch, pick up 6 more stitches along first short side, 12 stitches along first long side, 7 stitches along second short end, and 12 stitches along second long side—38 stitches.

Note: The next portion will be working in the round.

Round 1: Continuing in the same direction, knit in each stitch.
Round 2: Continuing in the same direction, knit 22 (26) stitches, bind off 4 (10) stitches (bed opening created), knit last 2 stitches—24 (28) stitches.

From here, you'll revert to working back and forth in rows.

Row 3: Working from right to left, knit around first short side, long side, and second short side.
Row 4: Working left to right, knit every stitch to opening as established.

Bind off.

For a video tutorial on binding off for this project, scan the QR code.

finishing

Weave in ends for a couple of inches (several centimeters), using your fingers. With needle and thread, securely tack down ends.

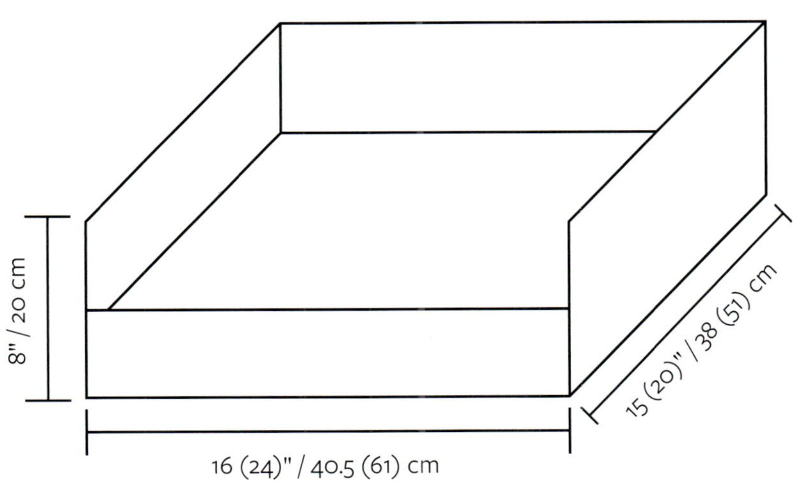

Trivetal

trivet/pot holder

Quick! You were just invited to a dinner and need a fast host gift! Enter Trivetal, a chunky pot holder with a handsome, contrasting fabric loop. This project is one of those that, although it's beginner level, looks chic because of its simplicity and mix of materials. Congratulations, you'll now be folks' favorite guest!

MATERIALS

- Super Bulky yarn (#6), 100% polyester (tube), in one color
  Shown: OMoiut Fluffy Big Twist (8.8 oz/250 g, 32 yd/29 m, 97% polyester/3% elastane): 1 skein
- ¾" (2 cm) x 4" (10 cm) piece of loop fabric (cork fabric, leather, or faux suede)
- 1 grommet
- Awl or leather punch
- Hand-sewing needle and coordinating thread (optional)

GAUGE

Approximately 4.5 stitches x 10 rows = 4" (10 cm) in garter stitch.

FINISHED MEASUREMENTS

9" (23 cm) square

trivet

Foundation Row: With A, chain 8 (or make a 9" chain).
Row 1: Working from right to left, pick up a loop in the 2nd stitch and every stitch to end of row—8 stitches
Row 2: Working from left to right, purl every stitch to end of row.
Row 3: Working from right to left, knit every stitch to end of row.
Row 4: Working from left to right, purl every stitch to end of row.

Repeat Rows 3–4 until piece measures 9" (23 cm), or when it is a square.

Bind off.

finishing

Weave in ends OR snip ends short and sew them to the back of the square.

CREATE LOOP

Using an awl or leather punch, make a hole in both ends of the fabric strip, about ½" (1.5 cm) up from the edge.

Fold the fabric piece over the top left-hand corner of the trivet. Following the grommet manufacturer's instructions, attach loop through both layers of the loop and the trivet.

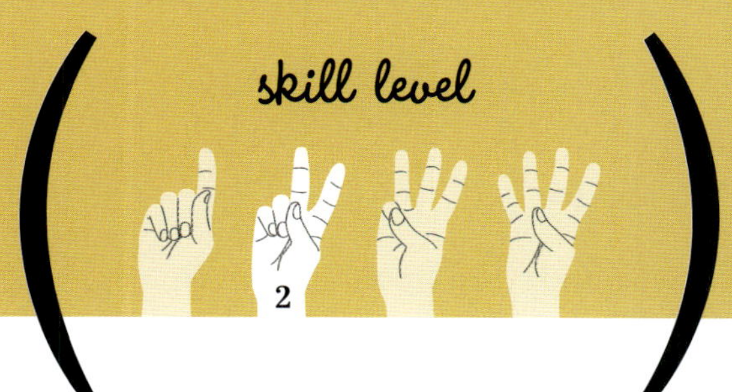

Coiled Over

spiral bowl-basket

Your bowl game is about to boil over with this project! By making long strands of cords and sewing them into place, you'll see this basket take shape before your eyes. Eye-catching home decor item with an organizational purpose: check!

MATERIALS

- Giant yarn (#8), 100% polyester (tube), in one color
  Shown: Big Twist Tubular (26.4 oz/750 g, 40 yd/37 m, 100% polyester): 1 ball Jade Green, Slime, or Varsity Blue
- Hand-sewing needle and coordinating thread

GAUGE

Not important for this project.

FINISHED MEASUREMENTS

13" (33 cm) wide
4" (10 cm) tall

note

This project is made by knitting long strands of i-cord (see page 20), then winding them into a coil to create the base. The side of the basket is created by sewing an additional strand around the perimeter of the base.

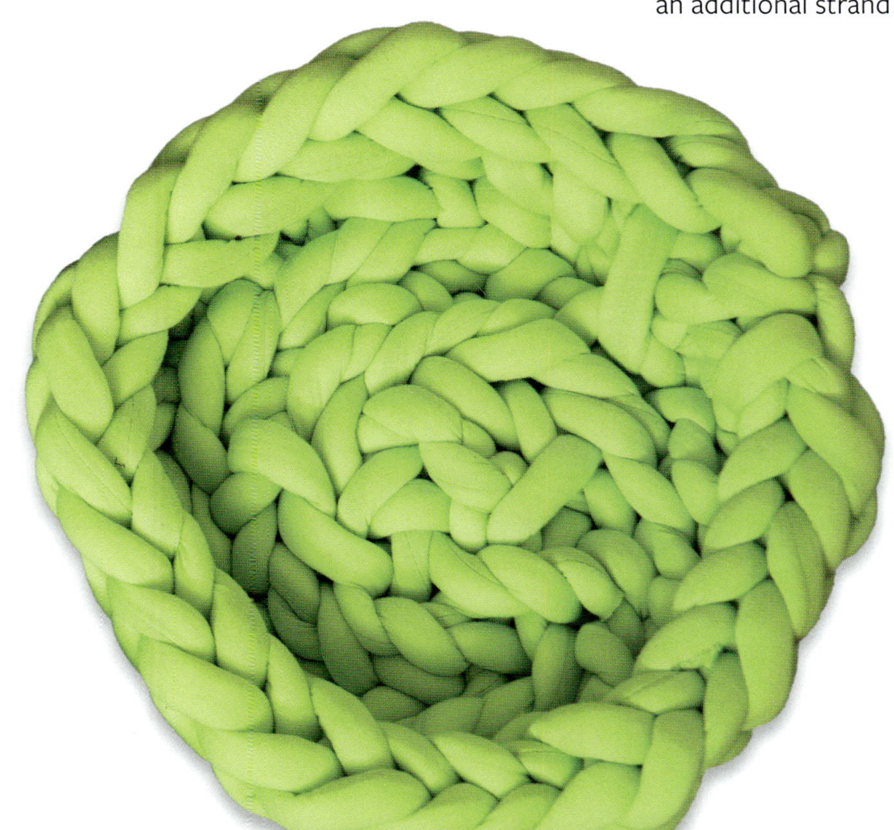

base

Foundation Row: Chain 2.
Row 1: Pull a loop up in the 2nd chain from hook—2 stitches.
Row 2: Bringing the strand from the left-hand side behind the live loops and knitting the rightmost stitch first, knit the stitches.
Row 3: Bringing the strand from the right-hand side behind the live loops and knitting the leftmost stitch first, knit the stitches.

I-cord pattern established.

Repeat Rows 2–3 until piece measures 60" (152 cm).

Bind off, leaving a few feet/about a meter of tail for seaming.

sides

Repeat as for base, binding off after about 30" (76 cm) and leaving at least an 18" (46 cm) tail.

finishing

ASSEMBLE BASE

Using your fingers, long tail, either mattress stitch or whipstitch, and illustration as a guide, wind piece into a spiral, sewing as you go. Once your i-cord is completely wound, *cut end so it's about 3" (8 cm) long. Pull out enough stuffing from the tube yarn so that you can neatly fold the outer fabric ends in. Using thread and needle, discreetly hand sew end to the piece so it's secure.**

ADD SIDES

Place the sides i-cord piece around the top of the outer edge of base. Using the tail, seam sides to base, ending by joining the two ends with a few stitches.

Repeat from * to ** for remaining tail.

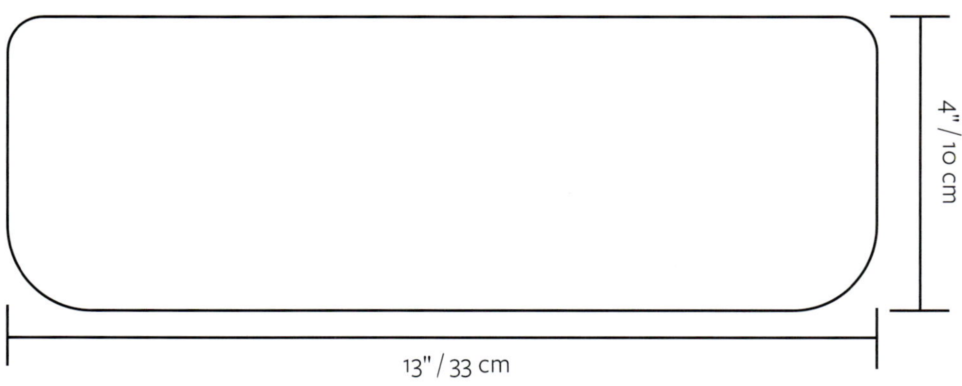

Scrappy

scrap yarn vase sleeve

Oh, how I love a Franken-project—one created out of a hodgepodge of yarns, shapes, and textures! I especially dig when said project *also* uses up some of those luscious yarn scraps that I couldn't bear to toss out. This vase sleeve is such a project. Its only purpose, gloriously, is to add cozy vibes and a few swishes of color to an otherwise plain home decor item. Let's get Scrappy!

MATERIALS

- Super Bulky (#6) yarn and/or Jumbo (#7) scraps—different types and textures are great!
- Yarn needle with an extra-large eye
- Vase or planter (desired size)
- Craft or binder clip (optional)

GAUGE

Not important for this project.

FINISHED MEASUREMENTS

Will vary

note

This project is completely customizable to fit any vase or planter. For reference, the vase shown has a circumference of 24" (60 cm) and is about 13" (33 cm) tall *before the top begins to curve*. All you need to know, though, is the bigger the vessel, the longer the knit strand will need to be to wrap around it. Have fun!

vase sleeve

Gather your favorite leftovers from other projects from this book, or elsewhere. Plan the order that you'll join new yarns (or go rogue, and grab as you go!)

Measure circumference of vase. Note that you'll need to finger knit the length of that circumference for every wrap you'd like around the piece you're covering. You can adjust this as you go, but it's good to at least have a ballpark number. For example, my finger-knit piece wraps around the vase approximately 5 times, 24" (60 cm) (circumference) x 5 wraps = 120" (300 cm) of knitting.

SLEEVE STRAND

With your first scrap, yarn wrap over 4 fingers—4 stitches.

Finger knit for as long as you'd like with the first color, join the next color; cut the last color.

Continue finger knitting, changing yarns at your whim [or every 7–14" (18–35.5 cm)] until piece is desired measurement.

Fasten off.

finishing

Weave in ends.

Using a yarn needle and a single strand of one of the smoother, thinner yarns in the bunch, begin wrapping the piece around the vessel. You may need a clip to hold it at first.

Begin whipstitching piece to itself, while it's on the vase. Continue wrapping and sewing as you go until finished.

QUARTZ

Frame in Lights

embellished picture frame

Those special moments deserve a little extra shine—embellish a frame with a hand-knit strand of lights. This project is a fun experiment with manipulated wire in an unexpected way. Stitch, glue, then bask in the glow!

MATERIALS

- 1 strand Ashland 55 ft/17 m (300 ct) LED String Lights (battery operated)
- 8" x 10" (20 x 25 cm) frame with stand [with at least 1.5" (4 cm) of coverable surface]
- Hot glue gun

GAUGE

The wire in light strands is highly pliable, making the gauge flexible. Gauge, however, is not important for this project.

FINISHED MEASUREMENTS

1 strand of lights makes an approximately 36" (91 cm) piece, which will fit the standard 8" x 10" (20 x 25 cm) frame.

frame embellishment

Foundation Row: Leaving a 6" (15 cm) tail for weaving, chain 2.
Row 1: Working from right to left, pull up a loop in the second chain—2 stitches.
Row 2: Working from left to right, knit every stitch to end of row.
Row 3: Working from right to left, knit every stitch to end of row.

Repeat Rows 2–3 until you have 36" (91 cm) (or as long as you need to go around the entire front of the frame).

Bind off. WITHOUT cutting wire, thread the wire with the battery pack through the final loop.

finishing

- Using the beginning tail and diagram as a guide, wrap the short end of the strand to the lower side of the opposite end.
- Lay the finished piece on the frame front so that the remaining wire and battery pack can be tucked behind the frame when it's standing. Manually shape piece to lie how you'd like it to on the frame front.
- Using the glue gun, SPARINGLY glue the piece to the frame—it may be helpful to hook a loop from a stitch around each corner.

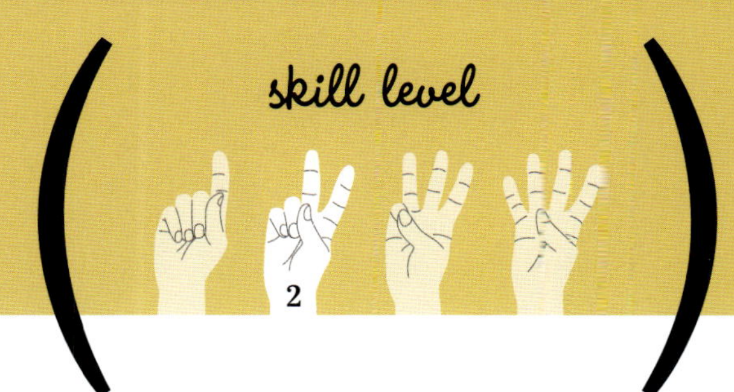

Weave, Not Waste

upcycled place mats

Let's rid the world of plastic grocery bags one craft at a time! For this project we'll transform these environmental enemies into picnic pals! These place mats are made of homemade (by you!) plastic yarn, called "plarn," that you knit into shape and embellish with simple weaving. The result is a reusable perch for your plates. Here's to *making* a difference!

MATERIALS

- Approximately 5 standard plastic grocery bags (for each mat)
- Scissors
- Rotary cutter, self-healing mat, and straightedge (optional)

GAUGE

Not important for this project.

FINISHED MEASUREMENTS

Approximately 13" x 16" (33 x 41 cm)
Note: Measurements may vary based on plarn strip consistency.

Make "Plarn" (Plastic Bag Yarn)

1. Lay bag on a flat surface.
2. Cut off handles and bag bottom.
3. Cut 2" (5 cm)-wide strips across the bag's width, leaving the sides of the bags uncut so you're creating loops.
4. To join "loop" strips, knot one through the end of the next as if it were fringe. Pull taut.
5. Wind plarn into a ball.

place mats

Foundation Row: Chain 7 [or as many as it takes to create a 13" (33 cm) piece].
Row 1: Working from right to left, pick up a loop (stitch) in the 2nd stitch and every stitch to end—7 stitches (or desired number).
Row 2: From left to right, knit every stitch to end of row.
Row 3: From right to left, knit every stitch to end of row.

Repeat Rows 2–3 until piece measures 16" (41 cm).

Bind off.

finishing

Weave in ends.

WOVEN STRIPS (OPTIONAL)

Cut 5 more bag-strip loops, this time also snipping one side to turn the loop into a longer strip.

Skipping outer stitch on either side, weave a strip over and under each of the rows of the center 5 stitches. Knot at each end. Slice ends to create fringe.

For a more advanced method of making plarn, scan the QR code.

Resources

levels key

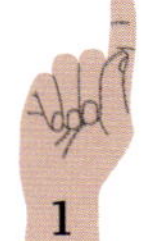

1 Finger
Super-simple project, perfect for first-timers or quick gifts.

2 Fingers
These projects might incorporate multiple stitch types or additional skills. With the tutorials, though, you've totally got this!

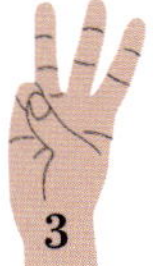

3 Fingers
You are a hand-knitting superstar, ready to play with multiple stitches and skills. I see you, superstar.

4 Fingers
You're basically a hand-knitting ninja. You're not afraid of big projects or nontraditional construction. High-five, or rather, four, maker!

For additional tips, tutorials, and bonus content, please scan the QR code to visit the No Needles Knitting Video Playlist.

yarn and supplies

Allred Leather Company
allredleathercompany.com

Amazon (Search for "Velvet Tube Yarn")
amazon.com

Bernat
yarnspirations.com

Etsy (Search for "Tube Yarn")
etsy.com

Knit Collage
knitcollage.com

Knit Picks
knitpicks.com

Lion Brand
lionbrand.com

Made Everyday (Zippered Pouch for Fur-bag Lining)
youtube.com/watch?v=i1AsfZRYlRM

Michaels (Big Twist, K+C, Loops & Threads)
michaels.com

Acknowledgments

Thanks to my editor, Joy Aquilino, for asking the question, "What's new in finger knitting?", which led me into a rabbit hole of discovering the hand-knitting trend. I was so inspired by the things that young makers are creating without the use of needles that it changed the trajectory of what this book became. Shout-out to project manager, Karen Julian, and copyeditor, Jean Bissell, for whipping this manuscript into shape. Thank you to Creative Director Regina Grenier for giving me so much creative freedom for this project. That is a gift rarely given, and I truly appreciate it.

A big shout-out to Jenny Bessonette and the Craft Yarn Council Standards Committee for approving the addition of a new yarn weight class, Giant 8. This inclusion supports setting up the success of hand and arm knitters using this book and beyond!

Anytime I can finagle working with people whom I love, the projects become even more special. For this book, I was so fortunate to be able to bring in the hands of a few of those folks.

Traci Goudie, thank you so much taking time off as a big-wig creative director to shoot another book for me. Your eye and skill make every project better. I'm so lucky to have you in my life and my work.

The opportunity to include two of my kids in this project boosted the joy for me. Thanks to Tristan Howell for your quick and efficient work (and sweet soul) on the schematics, and to Clover Campbell for your wonderful and whimsical illustrations (and your ride-or-die energy). I love you both more than all of the stitches ever knit in the world since the invention of craft.

To my MEOWers (knitting group of 20+ years), thanks for being my occasional, unwitting virtual companions while I made some of the projects in this book. You've been with me for every single one of my books, and welp, we pulled it off again!

Speaking of MEOWers, one of the group's members, Lori Steinberg, stepped in on a moment's notice to tech edit the patterns. Having someone I trust who's a text away to make the process quicker is invaluable!

Lastly, sending all of my love and appreciation to my husband, Dave Campbell, for supporting me through this and every project in life; to Tammy Crespo for being my emotional support human; and to my mom, Libby Bailey, for helping out with sample knitting for other professional commitments of mine so that I could focus on the projects in this book. Love, love, love you!

About the Author

Vickie Howell is an award-winning, Austin, Texas–based broadcaster, author, designer, and entrepreneur. Her career began as the host of the wildly popular DIY Network show *Knitty Gritty*.

Over the two decades since the show's inception—through various other television programs, YouTube videos, online courses, conference tours, books, a subscription box business, and the supportive, skill-building oasis Stitchwell Social Club—she has had the privilege of teaching hundreds of thousands of stitchers new yarn-y skills.

Vickie's mission is to empower people through community building and encourage them to lean into creativity by making DIY totally doable. Join her @vickiehowell.

index